新编基础汉语·写字篇

常用汉字部首

张朋朋
（Zhang Pengpeng）著

The Most
Common
Chinese Radicals

NEW
APPROACHES
TO LEARNING
CHINESE

First Edition   2001
Fourteenth Printing  2018

ISBN  978-7-80052-576-6

Copyright 2001 by Sinolingua Co., Ltd

Published by Sinolingua Co., Ltd

24 Baiwanzhuang Road, Beijing 100037, China

Tel: (86)10-68320585, 68997826

Fax: (86)10-68997826, 68326333

http://www.sinolingua.com.cn

E-mail: hyjx@sinolingua.com.cn

Facebook: www.facebook.com/sinolingua

Printed by Jinghua Hucais Printing Co., Ltd

*Printed in the People's Republic of China*

# 目 录

# Contents

# 前　言

对于外国人来说，学习和掌握汉语和汉字并不是一件非常困难的事情。过去，人们之所以不这样认为，主要是和教授这种语言和文字的方法不当有关。

过去，教授汉语和汉字一般是采用"语文一体"的方法，即"口语"和"文字"的教学同步进行。这种方法和教授英、法语等使用拼音文字的语言是一样的。本人认为："语文一体"的方法对于教授拼音文字的语言是合理和有效的，但用于教授汉语、汉字是不合适的，这是使外国人对学习汉语产生畏难情绪的主要原因。

一、汉字不是拼音文字。汉字是一种从象形文字发展而来的表意文字。汉字的形体不表示汉语的语音。因此，如果采用"语文一体"的方法，口语的内容用汉字来书写，将不利于学习者学习口语的发音，使汉字成为了他们学习口语的"绊脚石"。

二、汉字的字形是一个以一定数量的构件按照一定的规则进行组合的系统。因此，教学上，应先教这一定数量的构件及组合规则，然后再教由这些构件所组合的汉字。可是，"语文一体"的教法必然形成"文从语"的教学体系。也就是说，学什么话，教什么字。这种教法，汉字出现的顺序杂乱无章，体现不出汉字字形教学的系统性和规律性，从而大大增加了汉字教学的难度。

三、汉字具有构词性，有限的汉字构成了无限的词。"词"是由"字"构成的，知道了字音可以读出词音，知道了字义便于理解词义，"字"学的越多，会念的"词"就越多，学习"词"就越容易。也就是说，"识字量"决定了"识词量"。因此，汉语书面阅读教学应该以汉字作为教学的基本单位，应该把提高学习者的"识字量"作为教学的主要目标。"文从语"的做法恰恰是不可能做到这一点。因为，教材的编写从口语教学的要求和原则来考虑，自然要以"词"作为教学的基本单位。由于口语中能独立运用的最小的造句单位是"词"，所以在教"中国"一词时，必然只介绍"China"这一词义，而不会介绍"中"和"国"两个字的字义。中国语文教学历来是以"识字量"作为衡量一个人书面阅读能力强弱的标准，而"语文一体"这种教法等于是取消了汉字教学，从而大大影响了汉语书面阅读教学的效率。

综上所述，如果根据汉语和汉字的特点来对外国人进行基础汉语教学，在总体设计上就不应该采用"语文一体"的模式。我认为应该遵循以下几个原则来设计：

● 教学初期把"语"和"文"分开。

实现的方法是：口语教学主要借助汉语拼音来进行，对汉字不做要求。这样，使汉字不成其为"绊脚石"，使口语教学将变得极为容易。汉字教学另编教材，先进行汉字的字形教学，教材的内容从基本笔画入手，以部首为纲，以构件组合为核心。汉字字形教学和口语教学并行，这样，既有利于口语教学，又使汉字的字形教学具有了系统性和规律性。系统而有规律地进行汉字教学不仅可以大大降低学习的难度，而且从一开始就给了学习者一把开启神秘汉字大门的钥匙，这对他们是受益无穷的。

● 先进行口语教学和汉字字形教学，后进行识字阅读教学。

也就是说，对汉字的认读教学不要在初期阶段进行，而应安排在进行了一段口语和在结束了汉字字形教学之后。因为，具有了口语能力和书写汉字的技能对识字教学有促进作用，从而可以使学习者较为轻轻地跨越"识字"这第二道"门槛"。

● 阅读教学应以识字教学打头，采用独特的识字教学法。

"识字教学"和"写字教学"一样也是汉语教学中所独有的教学环节，应该根据汉字的特点编写适合外国人使用的识字课本。识字课本应以"字"作为教学的基本单位，以"以字组词"为核心，以快速提高学生的识字量和阅读能力为教学目标。

● 识字教学要和口语教学、阅读教学相结合。

具体做法是用所识的字和词编写口语对话体课文和叙述体散文作为这一阶段教材的内容。这一阶段的教学在程序上是一环扣一环的，在练习方式上是一种有听、有说、有读、有写的综合式教学。

上述总体设计图示：

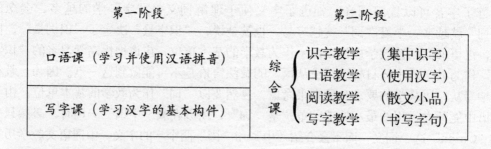

| 第一阶段 | 第二阶段 |
|---|---|
| 口语课（学习并使用汉语拼音） | 综合课 识字教学（集中识字） 口语教学（使用汉字） |
| 写字课（学习汉字的基本构件） | 阅读教学（散文小品） 写字教学（书写字句） |

根据上述原则，本人编写了一套基础汉语教程。本教程包括三本教材：
一是口语篇，书名是《口语速成》。此书用于口语课。
二是写字篇，书名是《常用汉字部首》。此书用于写字课。
三是识字篇，书名是《集中识字》。此书用于综合课。

使用这套教材，初学者先学习《口语速成》和《常用汉字部首》，学完之后再学习《识字课本》，就像吃西餐一样，一道菜一道菜来，循序渐进。这样，学习者不仅不会觉得汉语难学，而且还会被汉字的文化内涵和艺术魅力所深深吸引。

张朋朋

# Introduction

The Chinese language has, for too long, been perceived as being beyond the grasp of foreign learners. This misconception can mostly be contributed to improper teaching methods.

For several decades, the spoken and written forms of the Chinese language have been taught simultaneously to beginners. This is a fine approach for teaching Western languages such as French or English, which employ a phonetic system or alphabet as an aid to learning pronunciation, but it is certainly not suited to teaching spoken and written Chinese. The reasons for this are threefold:

1. Chinese characters cannot be read phonetically. Chinese characters developed from pictographs into ideographs; meaning there is no direct relationship between the form and structure of Chinese characters and their pronunciation. Therefore, teaching both spoken and written Chinese at the beginning stages of language acquisition will not help foreign learners to master pronunciation. In such a situation the characters will, if anything, only act as a stumbling block to the acquisition of oral fluency.

2. Each Chinese character is made up of components that follow a specific stroke order and rules of formation; it then follows that simple components should be taught first, progressing to more complicated components and whole characters. But in the approach of teaching spoken and written Chinese simultaneously, spoken items are followed by a corresponding written character. Obviously, in this approach, the characters are not chosen systematically according to their structural compositions, so the rules that govern the writing of characters are not reflected, making the teaching and learning of characters only more chaotic and difficult.

3. Chinese characters form the basis of courses in reading. Single syllable characters can be combined to make various disyllabic or multi-syllabic words. There are unlimited combinations that can be made by adding different components to characters to change or expand meanings. If a learner is able to pronounce some characters or character components, it follows that the learner would be able to read the words they form, or at least infer meaning from context. Knowing the meaning of certain characters will aid learners in understanding the meaning of the words they represent, and as they learn more characters and character components, their ability to read will increases; learning words thus becomes easier. Since character recognition determines word recognition, the main objective in teaching Chinese characters should be to raise the learner's level of character recognition.

However, this is not possible with the "writing following speaking" approach. When teaching colloquial Chinese, words are used instead of characters as the basis of teaching, because the word is the smallest meaning-based unit in basic sentence construction. When teaching the word 中国, for example, we will invariably explain its meaning with the English word "China", but the two characters that form the word, 中 "middle", and 国 "kingdom", are not explicitly identified. Traditionally, Chinese language teaching methods has always used "character recognition" as the criterion in judging a learner's ability to read texts. The "writing following speaking" approach simply disregards the necessity of teaching characters on their own and does not give the characters the place they deserve, thus greatly reducing the efficiency of teaching written Chinese.

Our new approach may be summarized as follows:

● In the initial stage of learning, spoken Chinese and character recognition and writing will be taught separately.

● Teaching materials for oral lessons will mainly use a system of romanization called *Hanyu pinyin*, so the learners are not required to deal with characters during their oral lessons. There are obvious reasons for this; learning to speak Chinese becomes easier for Western second language learners when a phonetic system of romanization is used to represent Chinese words.

● When teaching spoken Chinese the form of Chinese characters will be introduced systematically: first strokes, then radicals, and finally structural components. These "stumbling blocks" will then become easier to navigate, thus giving learners the tools necessary for later stages of character identification.

● After the learner is able to speak and has learned the form and structure of characters they will be taught to read characters using specially designed texts, focusing on character recognition and word formation, with the aim of quickly enlarging vocabulary and acquiring a basic reading ability.

● In the reading stage, character learning will be combined with continuous spoken language training and reading aptitude training. Texts will be in the form of dialogues and narrative prose pieces written with the characters learned in each lesson, as to offer concise and easy-to-read learning material. The exercises will include comprehensive forms of listening, speaking, reading, and writing that are closely linked and complementary.

What is discussed above can be illustrated as below:

|  Initial stage  |  Second stage  |
| --- | --- |
| **Oral Course**<br>Learn to use pinyin | **Comprehensive Course**<br>Character learning: intensive training<br>Oral training: application of characters<br>Reading: proses, etc.<br>Writing: characters and sentences |
| **Writing Course**<br>Learn the basic structural components<br>of characters | |

Based on the above methods, *New Approaches to Learning Chinese* has been devised, which includes three textbooks:

**Intensive Spoken Chinese** (oral course)

Includes 40 conversational lessons, approximately 1,000 commonly used words, and numerous grammatical notes.

**The Most Common Chinese Radicals** (writing course)

Contains approximately 100 Chinese radicals, and information on the basic structure of Chinese characters.

**Rapid Literacy in Chinese** (comprehensive course)

Employs 750 commonly used Chinese characters and 1,300 words formed from them to make 25 short sentences, 25 conversational dialogues, and 4 narrative prose pieces.

Beginners who have completed *Intensive Spoken Chinese* and *The Most Common Chinese Radicals* will then proceed to *Rapid Literacy in Chinese*. Progressing step-by-step through the Chinese language will help learners to acquire Chinese language skills with an ease never before thought possible. In addition to learning the language itself, there is much that can be learned about Chinese culture from Chinese characters, besides their alluring charm and fascination, which will aid learners in navigating both the language and Chinese society itself.

Zhang Pengpeng

# 编 写 体 例

　　本书是一本为外国人编写的学习书写汉字的基础教材。

　　汉字是有一定结构规律的文字，它是以一定数量的构件按照一定的规则进行组合的，有其完整的系统性。也就是说，成千上万个汉字是由少量的构件有规律地组合而成的。英文的所有单词都是由26个字母组合而成的。汉字以构件组字和英文以字母组词不同：一、汉字的构件数量比英文字母要多，大约300多个，常用构件有100多个。二、汉字以构件组字不是线形排列，而是在一个方框内以上下、左右、内外等方式拼合而成。三、汉字构件的拼合具有逻辑性，也就是说，它与字义有着密切的关系。因此，学习汉字只要掌握了这少量的最基本的构件和汉字的组合规则，就可以书写几乎所有的汉字了。这样学习，不仅节省时间，而且也有利于对字义和字形的记忆。

　　根据上述认识，本书的编写体例确定为从笔画入手，以部首为纲，以构件组合为核心。

## 一、从笔画入手

　　汉字的构件是由笔画构成的。因此学习汉字构件要从笔画入手。本书共介绍了8个基本笔画。对每个笔画还介绍了它的几种变形写法以及笔画的名称和笔顺规则。

## 二、以部首为纲

　　汉字在结构上分两大类，一类是独体字，一类是合体字。独体字又分象形字和指事字，合体字又分会意字和形声字。合体字是由独体字或由独体字演变来的偏旁构成的。汉字的部首一般是独体字或由独体字演变而来的偏旁，所以，部首本身可以说是汉字最基本的构件。另外，部首往往又是合体字中会意字的偏旁和形声字的形旁，所以，以部首为纲教汉字，便于对合体字中的会意字和形声字进行结构上分析和字义上的说明。汉语的工具书和词典多是以部首来检字。以部首为纲来编写此书的另一个目的是想为学习者将来使用汉语工具书打下一个坚实的基础。

　　本书共介绍了108个最常用的部首，按照由易到难，即从笔画少到笔画多的顺序排列。对每个部首，本书介绍了它的名称、意义、作用、来源以及它的写法和笔画数等多项内容。

## 三、以部件组合为核心

　　在每个部首下介绍几个带有同一偏旁的合体字。对每个合体字不仅介绍了它的字音、字义，而且突出介绍了它和构件之间的逻辑关系以及构件组合的结构类型。

# To the User

This book introduces to foreign learners the basics of acquiring and writing Chinese characters in the most efficient way.

Chinese characters initially developed from pictographs formed in a standard manner with a certain number of components that are comparable to the 26 letters in the modern English alphabet. However, these components are different from the letters in the English alphabet in several ways: the components are much larger in number (about 300, in which over 100 are in common use), and the components are not arranged in a horizontal line but in other forms such as upper-lower, left-right, and inside-outside. Therefore, once learners understand these basic components and the rules for arranging them, they can write almost all Chinese characters. This is not only a time saving approach, it is also an easy way to remember the form and meaning of a character.

The format of the lessons is as follows:

## 1. Starting from the most basic strokes

All character components are formed from basic strokes with which learners must first become familiar. The book introduces the eight basic strokes, with the variant forms, stroke names, and the rules for forming them.

## 2. Learning the characters through radicals

Structurally, Chinese characters can be classified into two groups: one-component characters, and compound characters. The first group can be further categorized into pictograms and indicative characters, and the second group, into associative characters and picto-phonograms. Compound characters are composed of one-component characters or components evolved from them, with such components generally constituting the radicals. Therefore, radicals can be taken as the most basic components of Chinese characters. In addition, radicals also act as meaning-based components in associative characters and picto-phonograms. Thus, teaching characters through radicals makes it easier to analyze the structure and meaning of picto-phonograms and associative characters. As almost all Chinese dictionaries use radical indexing systems for characters, it is essential to prepare learners for the use of such dictionaries.

To these ends, the 108 most commonly used radicals are introduced in this text, sequenced from simple to complicated according to the number of strokes in each radical. Each radical is accompanied by its name, meaning, function, origin, stroke order, and number of strokes.

## 3. Focusing on the combination of components

Accompanying each radical are several compound characters containing the radical itself. As well, the pronunciation and meaning of each compound character is given. Emphasis is placed on the logical relationship between the character's components, meaning, and structure.

◆ 笔画　　bǐhuà　　strokes

汉字数量虽多，但都是由二十几种笔画构成的。在这二十几种笔画中最基本的有八种，其余的十几种是在这八种基础上有不同程序的变化。本书第一至第八页介绍基本笔画。

Although there are many Chinese characters, there are only about 20 kinds of strokes used to form them. Among these however, it is only necessary to learn the eight most important strokes and view the others as their variants. See pages 1-8 for the basic strokes.

◆ 笔顺　　bǐshùn　　stroke order

在书写一个汉字时，有的笔画先写，有的后写，是有一定顺序的，这就是笔顺。如：

In writing Chinese characters, one should follow a certain order of the strokes, i.e. some strokes precede others, e.g.

◆ 笔顺规则　　bǐshùn guīzé　　rules of stroke order

笔顺规则是指独体字哪一笔先写，哪一笔后写的规则。本书在介绍基本笔画的同时也介绍了几条笔顺规则。参见第一至第八页。书写合体字要遵循结构顺序规则，有关结构顺序规则，本书在介绍合体字时用图来表示，如：

The rules of stroke order specify that in a one-component character, certain strokes should precede others. This is elaborated on pages 1-8 while introducing the eight basic strokes. In writing compound-component characters, one should follow the structural order, which is explained through diagrams as follows, e.g.

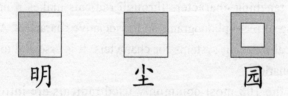

明　　　　尘　　　　园

◆ 笔画数　　bǐhuàshù　　stroke numbers

构成一个汉字的笔画数量叫笔画数，如"大"字是三画。查字典时需要知道笔画数。

The stroke number is the total number of strokes that compose a Chinese character, e.g. 大 has three strokes. This is basic knowledge necessary for consulting a dictionary.

| 一 | 十 | 大 |  | 3 |

◆ 独体字　　dútǐzì　　one-component characters

独体字是由笔画组成的、不能再分成两部分的字，如："人""木"，"日""月"。独体字有两种，一种是象形字，一种是指事字。

One-component characters have only one basic part and cannot be subdivided, e.g. 人, 木, 日, 月. One-component characters have two categories: pictograms and indicative characters.

人　　木　　日　　月

◆ 象形字　　xiàngxíngzì　　pictograms

字的形状像所表示的具体事物的独体字叫象形字。如："人""口""木""日""月"等。独体字中象形字占大多数。

Pictograms represent in stylized form the objects they refer to, e.g. 人, 口, 木, 日, 月. A great part of the one-component characters are pictograms.

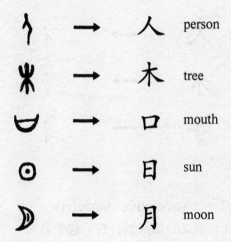

◆ 指事字　　zhǐshìzì　　indicative characters

用笔画的组合揭示出某种抽象意义的独体字叫指事字，如："上""下""中"等。

Strokes can be combined to show an abstract meaning. One-component characters composed in this way are called indicative characters, e.g. 上, 下, 中.

上 above　　　　　下 under　　　　　中 among

◆ 合体字　　hétǐzì　　compound characters

合体字是由两个或两个以上部分组成的字，如："从""众""休""河"。

Characters composed of two or more parts are called compound characters, e.g. 从, 众, 休, 河.

从　　众　　休　　河

◆ 偏旁　　piānpáng　　components

构成合体字的部分叫偏旁。偏旁有两种，一种是独体字，一种是由独体字演变来的符号，如："亻"就是由"人"演变来的。偏旁在合体字中有时表音，有时表义。表义的偏旁叫形旁，表音的偏旁叫声旁。

The parts which form the compound characters are called components. The components are either one-component characters themselves or symbols derived from them, e.g. 亻 is a symbol derived from the pictogram 人. Some components show meaning; others indicate sound.

人　→　亻

水　→　氵

手　→　扌

◆ 会意字　　huìyìzì　　associative characters

由两个或两个以上的具有意义的偏旁组合在一起来表示一个新的意义的合体字叫会意字。如："明""尘"。

Associative characters come from the combination of two or more meaningful components to create a new character with a new meaning, e.g. 明, 尘.

日　＋　月　＝　明
sun　　　moon　　　bright

小　＋　土　＝　尘
small　　　soil　　　dust

◆ 形声字　　xíngshēngzì　　picto-phonograms

构成合体字的偏旁，一个表义，一个表音，这种合体字叫形声字。如："妈"。合体字中大部分是形声字。

Picto-phonograms are a kind of compound characters, with one component indicating its meaning, the other indicating its pronunciation, e.g. 妈. Most of the compound characters are picto-phonograms.

$$ 女 \quad + \quad 马 \quad = \quad 妈 $$

| woman | horse | mother |
|---|---|---|
| semantic part | phonetic part | mā |

◆ 部首　　bùshǒu　　radicals

汉语字典根据汉字形体的偏旁分成不同的门类，如"口部""人部"等。口部中的字都有"口"字旁，人部中的字都含有"人"字旁。这些偏旁就叫做"部首"。

In Chinese dictionaries, the characters are arranged according to the different category of components, e.g. 口部, 人部. All the characters in 口部 contain the component 口, and all the characters in 人部 contain the component 人. These components are called radicals.

【口部】　kǒubù　the radical mouth　喝 唱 叫 吃 喊 听

【人部】　réubù　the radical person　从 众 个 合 介

◆ 汉字结构　　Hànzì jiégòu　　character structure

汉字结构是指合体字的结构。合体字的结构类型主要有三种，即左右结构、上下结构、内外结构。如："林""明""好"是左右结构。"男""尘""尖""忘"是上下结构。"回""国""园"等是内外结构。

The structures of the compound characters are divided into three principal types: left-right structure, top-bottom structure, and inside-outside structure, e.g.

林　明　好　　　　left-right structure

男　尘　尖　　　　top-bottom structure

回　国　园　　　　inside-outside structure

| | | | | | | | |
|---|---|---|---|---|---|---|---|
| 一 | horizontal | 土 | soil | 贝 | seashell | 羊 | sheep |
| 丨 | vertical | 弓 | bow | 车 | vehicle | 页 | head |
| 丿 | left-falling | 口 | square | 戈 | dagger-axe | 衣 | clothes |
| 丶 | right-falling | 巾 | towel | 斤 | axe | [衤] | clothes |
| 乛 | turning | 辶 | walk | 气 | air | 竹 | bamboo |
| 乚 | hook | 马 | horse | 欠 | yawn | 自 | self |
| 丶 | dot | 宀 | roof | 犬 | dog | 老 | old |
| ノ | rising | 女 | woman | [犭] | dog | 走 | walking |
| 人 | person | 尸 | corpse | 文 | script | 身 | body |
| 亻 | person | 彡 | ornament | 王 | king or jade | 豕 | pig |
| 刀 | knife | 广 | wide | 心 | heart | 言 | speech |
| 刂 | knife | 门 | door | [忄] | heart | [讠] | speech |
| 力 | strength | 夕 | sunset | 歹 | evil | 足 | leg, foot |
| 儿 | son | 攵 | hand holding a stick | 穴 | hole | 𧾷 | leg, foot |
| 冫 | ice | | | 目 | eye | 金 | gold, metals |
| 又 | right hand | 户 | single door | 田 | field | [钅] | metals |
| 辶 | structure | 毛 | hair | 禾 | cereal | 鱼 | fish |
| 厂 | factory | 爪 | claw | 白 | white | 雨 | rain |
| 卩 | single ear | 爫 | claw | 立 | standing up | 食 | food |
| 阝 | mound, town | 木 | tree, wood | 疒 | sickness | [饣] | food |
| 大 | big | 片 | flat | 皿 | receptacle | 革 | leather |
| 纟 | silk | 父 | father | 石 | stone | 黑 | black |
| 工 | work | 牛 | ox | 示 | show | | |
| 彳 | step with the left foot | 牜 | cattle | [礻] | show | | |
| 子 | child | 日 | sun | 鸟 | bird | | |
| 孑 | child | 月 | moon | 母 | mother | | |
| 口 | mouth | 手 | hand | 舟 | boat | | |
| 山 | mountain | [扌] | hand | 虫 | insect | | |
| 艹 | grass | 火 | fire | 耳 | ear | | |
| 小 | small | 灬 | fire | 虍 | tiger | | |
| ⺌ | small | 水 | water | 米 | rice | | |
| | | [氵] | water | 西 | west | | |

# 【笔画】

"一"是部首，有两个变体。"一"的写法是：从左到右，要平。
The horizontal stroke is a radical with two variant forms. Execute from left to right levelly.

一　　名称：横

Name: héng　　　　　　　horizontal

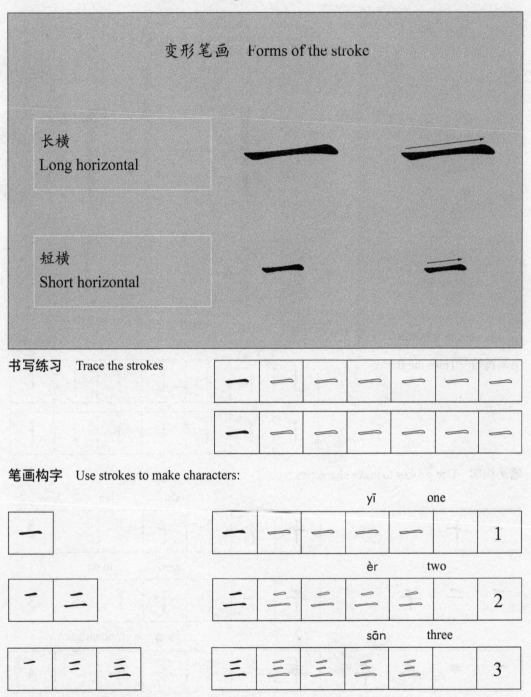

变形笔画　Forms of the stroke

长横
Long horizontal

短横
Short horizontal

书写练习　Trace the strokes

笔画构字　Use strokes to make characters:

一

yī　　　one

一　一　一　一　一　　1

一　二

èr　　　two

二　二　二　二　二　　2

一　二　三

sān　　　three

三　三　三　三　三　　3

笔顺规则：从上到下　　　　Order: From top to bottom

1

# 【笔画】

丨　　　名称：竖

　　　　　Name: shù　　　　　vertical

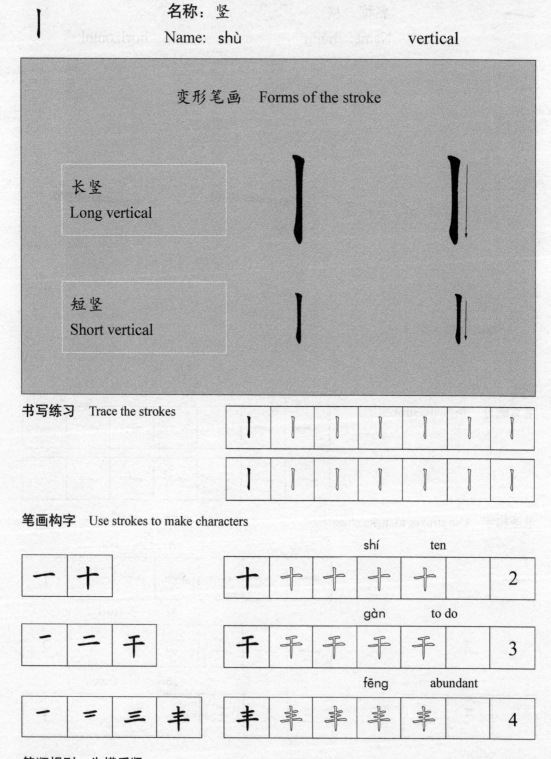

变形笔画　Forms of the stroke

长竖
Long vertical

短竖
Short vertical

书写练习　Trace the strokes

笔画构字　Use strokes to make characters

一　十

shí　　ten
十　十　十　十　十　　2

一　二　干

gàn　　to do
干　干　干　干　干　　3

一　二　三　丰

fēng　　abundant
丰　丰　丰　丰　丰　　4

笔顺规则：先横后竖　　　　Order: Horizontal before vertical

2

# 【笔画】

"丿"是部首，有两个变体。"丿"的写法是：从上向左下，成弧形。
The left-falling stroke is also a radical with two variant forms. Execute from top to lower left, as an arc (curve).

丿

名称：撇

Name: piě                    left-falling

变形笔画　Forms of the stroke

| 横撇 Level left-falling | |
| 竖撇 Vertical left-falling | |

书写练习　Trace the strokes

丿 丿 丿 丿 丿 丿 丿

丿 丿 丿 丿 丿 丿 丿

笔画构字　Use strokes to make characters

| ノ | 二 | 千 |

qiān    thousand

| 千 | 千 | 千 | 千 | 千 | | 3 |

| 丿 | ⸍ | ⸗ | 午 |

wǔ    noon

| 午 | 午 | 午 | 午 | 午 | | 4 |

| 丿 | 刂 | 川 |

chuān    river

| 川 | 川 | 川 | 川 | 川 | | 3 |

笔顺规则：从左到右                Order: From left to right

3

# 【笔画】

"捺"有两个变体。"捺"的写法是：从上向右下，成弧形。
The right-falling stroke has two variant forms. Write from top to lower right, as an arc (curve).

丶

名称：捺

Name: nà                        right-falling

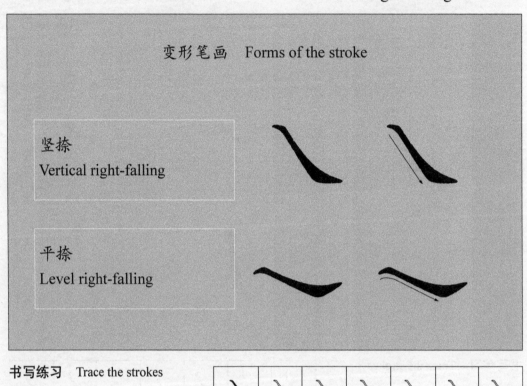

变形笔画　Forms of the stroke

竖捺
Vertical right-falling

平捺
Level right-falling

书写练习　Trace the strokes

笔画构字　Use strokes to make characters

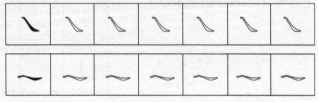

| ノ | 八 |
|---|---|

bā　　eight

| 八 | 八 | 八 | 八 | 八 | | 2 |

| ノ | 入 |
|---|---|

rù　　to enter

| 入 | 入 | 入 | 入 | 入 | | 2 |

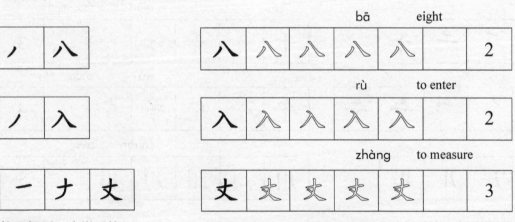

| 一 | 亅 | 丈 |
|---|---|---|

zhàng　　to measure

| 丈 | 丈 | 丈 | 丈 | 丈 | | 3 |

笔顺规则：先撇后捺

Order: Left-falling before right-falling

4

# 【笔画】

フ

名称：折

Name: zhé          turning

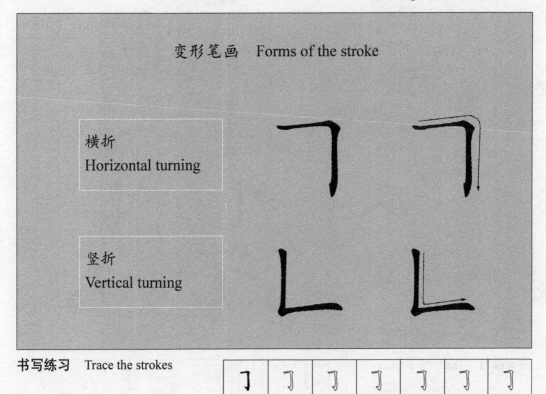

变形笔画   Forms of the stroke

横折
Horizontal turning

竖折
Vertical turning

书写练习   Trace the strokes

笔画构字   Use strokes to make characters

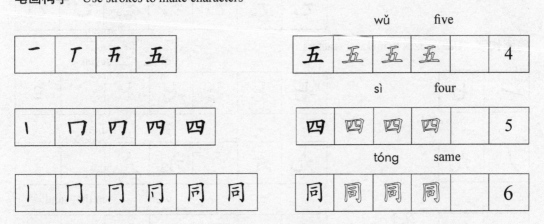

| wǔ | five |
| sì | four |
| tóng | same |

笔顺规则：先外后内          Order: From outside to inside

# 【笔画】

し

名称:钩

Name: gōu　　　　　　hook

变形笔画　Forms of the stroke

竖钩
Vertical hook

竖右弯钩
Vertical right hook

横折右弯钩
Horizontal right hook

</br>

**书写练习**　Trace the strokes

| 亅 | 亅 | 亅 | 亅 | 亅 | 亅 | 亅 |
|---|---|---|---|---|---|---|

| し | し | し | し | し | し | し | し |
|---|---|---|---|---|---|---|---|

| 乙 | 乙 | 乙 | 乙 | 乙 | 乙 | 乙 |
|---|---|---|---|---|---|---|

**笔画构字**　Use strokes to make characters

| 一 | 七 |
|---|---|

qī　　seven

| 七 | 七 | 七 | 七 | 七 | | 2 |
|---|---|---|---|---|---|---|

| 丿 | 九 |
|---|---|

jiǔ　　nine

| 九 | 九 | 九 | 九 | 九 | | 2 |
|---|---|---|---|---|---|---|

| 一 | 丆 | 万 |
|---|---|---|

wàn　　ten thousand

| 万 | 万 | 万 | 万 | 万 | | 3 |
|---|---|---|---|---|---|---|

# 【笔画】

"点"是部首，有两个变体。写法：向右下方点，或向左下方点。
The dot stroke is a radical with two variant forms. Write the dot toward lower right or left.

、 名称：点

Name: diǎn  dot

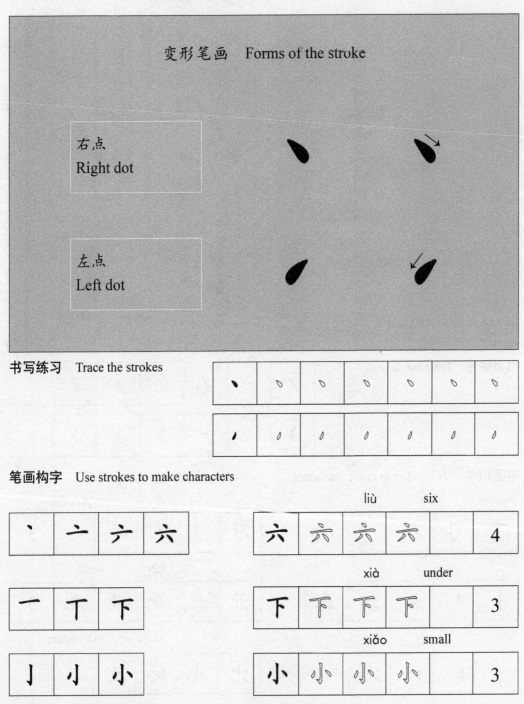

变形笔画  Forms of the stroke

右点
Right dot

左点
Left dot

书写练习  Trace the strokes

笔画构字  Use strokes to make characters

liù  six

、 二 六 六 | 六 六 六 六 | 4

xià  under

一 丁 下 | 下 下 下 下 | 3

xiǎo  small

亅 亅 小 | 小 小 小 小 | 3

笔顺规则：先中间后两边   Order: Middle before the two sides

7

# 【笔画】

"提"有两个变体。写法：一个从下向右上提，一个先竖后提。
The rising stroke has two variant forms. Execute the first from bottom to upper right and the other vertical then rising.

✓

**名称：提**

Name: tí          rising

变形笔画   Forms of the stroke

**上提**
Rising

**竖提**
Vertical and rising

书写练习   Trace the strokes

| / | / | / | / | / | / | / |
|---|---|---|---|---|---|---|

| ∠ | ∠ | ∠ | ∠ | ∠ | ∠ | ∠ |
|---|---|---|---|---|---|---|

笔画构字   Use strokes to make characters

| 丁 | 习 | 习 |
|---|---|---|

xí      to practise

| 习 | 习 | 习 | 习 | 3 |
|---|---|---|---|---|

| 丨 | 十 | 才 | 才 | 北 |
|---|---|---|---|---|

běi      north

| 北 | 北 | 北 | 北 | 5 |
|---|---|---|---|---|

| 一 | ヒ | ヒ | 比 |
|---|---|---|---|

bǐ      to compare

| 比 | 比 | 比 | 比 | 4 |
|---|---|---|---|---|

# 【人部】

人部的字多和人有关。人字旁的位置一般在字的上部，也有在两侧的。
Characters with the radical 人 mostly are relevant to human beings. It is usually placed at the top or on either side.

人　　rén　　　　　　　　　　　person

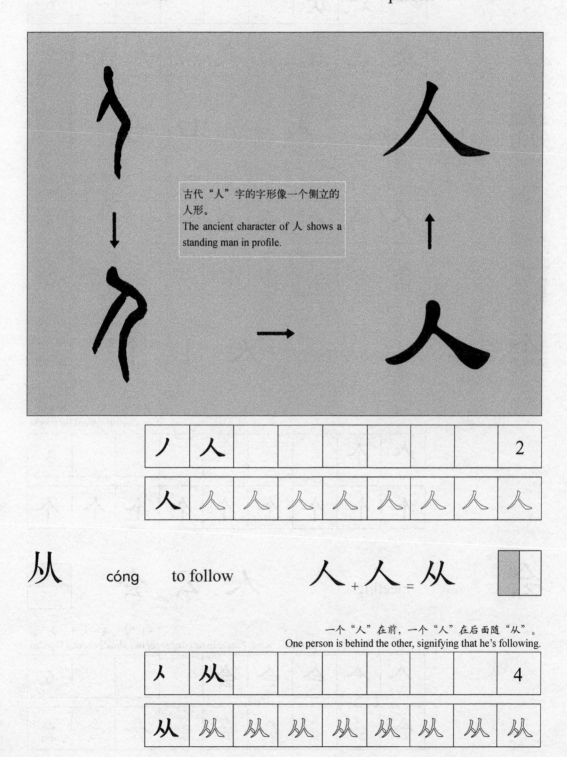

古代"人"字的字形像一个侧立的人形。
The ancient character of 人 shows a standing man in profile.

| 丿 | 人 |  |  |  |  |  |  | 2 |
|---|---|---|---|---|---|---|---|---|
| 人 | 人 | 人 | 人 | 人 | 人 | 人 | 人 | 人 |

从　　cóng　　to follow　　　　人 + 人 = 从

一个"人"在前，一个"人"在后面随"从"。
One person is behind the other, signifying that he's following.

| 人 | 从 |  |  |  |  |  |  | 4 |
|---|---|---|---|---|---|---|---|---|
| 从 | 从 | 从 | 从 | 从 | 从 | 从 | 从 | 从 |

**众** zhòng crowd 人 + 人 + 人 = 众

三人"人"在一起表示人多，人多是"众"。
Three 人 shows a large number of people.

| 人 | 众 | 众 | | | | | 6 |
|---|---|---|---|---|---|---|---|

| 众 | 众 | 众 | 众 | 众 | 众 | 众 | 众 | 众 |
|---|---|---|---|---|---|---|---|---|

**合** hé to close 人 + 一 + 口 = 合

"口"表示"人"的嘴，嘴"合"起来后成"一"条缝。
口 shows a mouth. The closed lips are like a crack, 一.

| 人 | 人 | 仐 | 合 | 合 | | | 6 |
|---|---|---|---|---|---|---|---|

| 合 | 合 | 合 | 合 | 合 | 合 | 合 | 合 | 合 |
|---|---|---|---|---|---|---|---|---|

**个** gè (a measure word) 人 + 丨 = 个

"个"是用于表示"人"的量词。
个 is a measure word for people.

| 人 | 个 | | | | | | 3 |
|---|---|---|---|---|---|---|---|

| 个 | 个 | 个 | 个 | 个 | 个 | 个 | 个 | 个 |
|---|---|---|---|---|---|---|---|---|

**会** huì meeting 人 + 云 = 会

"人"们"云"集一起开"会"。
云 means cloud. People in meeting seem like clouds coming together.

| 人 | 人 | 会 | 会 | 会 | | | 6 |
|---|---|---|---|---|---|---|---|

| 会 | 会 | 会 | 会 | 会 | 会 | 会 | 会 | 会 |
|---|---|---|---|---|---|---|---|---|

# 【亻部】

"亻"是由"人"字演变而来的。亻部的字多和人的活动有关。立人旁的位置在字的左侧。
亻is evolved from 人. Characters with the radical 亻mostly refer to the activities of human beings. It is placed on the left side.

亻

称说：单立人

Name: dānlìrén　　　　person

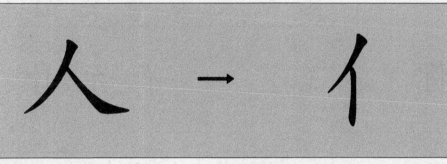

笔顺及笔画数　Stroke order and number

| ノ | 亻 | | 2 |
|---|---|---|---|

| 亻 | 亻 | 亻 | 亻 | 亻 |
|---|---|---|---|---|

休　xiū　to rest

"木"表示一棵树，"人"靠着树在"休"息。
木 shows a tree. A person rests by leaning against a tree.

| 亻 | 亻 | 什 | 仃 | 休 | | 6 |
|---|---|---|---|---|---|---|

| 休 | 休 | 休 | 休 | 休 | 休 | 休 | 休 | 休 |
|---|---|---|---|---|---|---|---|---|

体　tǐ　body

亻 + 本 = 体

身"体"是"人"之根"本"。
本 means root. The body is the root of every human being.

| 亻 | 亻 | 什 | 仃 | 休 | 体 | 7 |
|---|---|---|---|---|---|---|

| 体 | 体 | 体 | 体 | 体 | 体 | 体 | 体 | 体 |
|---|---|---|---|---|---|---|---|---|

# 他 tā he

イ + 也 = 他

"他"是"人"称代词。
"He" is a personal pronoun.

| イ | 亻 | 仂 | 他 | | | | 5 |
|---|---|---|---|---|---|---|---|
| 他 | 他 | 他 | 他 | 他 | 他 | 他 | 他 | 他 |

# 你 nǐ you

イ + 尔 = 你

"你"是"人"称代词。
"You" is a personal pronoun.

| イ | 亻 | 伫 | 佇 | 你 | 你 | | 7 |
|---|---|---|---|---|---|---|---|
| 你 | 你 | 你 | 你 | 你 | 你 | 你 | 你 | 你 |

# 们 men (plural suffix)

イ + 门 = 们

"们"在"人"称代词后表示复数。
们 is used after a personal pronoun to form a plural.

| イ | 亻 | 伫 | 们 | | | | 5 |
|---|---|---|---|---|---|---|---|
| 们 | 们 | 们 | 们 | 们 | 们 | 们 | 们 | 们 |

# 作 zuò to write; work

イ + 乍 = 作

"作"事情是"人"的活动。
Doing a work is a person's activity.

| イ | 亻 | 仁 | 仁 | 作 | 作 | | 7 |
|---|---|---|---|---|---|---|---|
| 作 | 作 | 作 | 作 | 作 | 作 | 作 | 作 | 作 |

# 【刀部】

刀　　　　　dāo　　　　　　　　　　knife

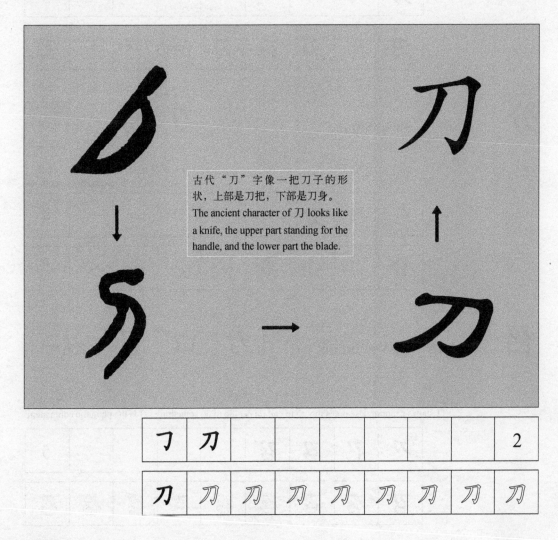

古代"刀"字像一把刀子的形状，上部是刀把，下部是刀身。
The ancient character of 刀 looks like a knife, the upper part standing for the handle, and the lower part the blade.

| フ | 刀 |  |  |  |  |  |  | 2 |
|---|---|---|---|---|---|---|---|---|
| 刀 | 刀 | 刀 | 刀 | 刀 | 刀 | 刀 | 刀 | 刀 |

切　　qiē　　to cut　　　　　　⼟ + 刀 = 切　

"切"东西要使用"刀"子。
We use a knife to cut something.

| 一 | ⼟ | 切 |  |  |  |  |  | 4 |
|---|---|---|---|---|---|---|---|---|
| 切 | 切 | 切 | 切 | 切 | 切 | 切 | 切 | 切 |

# 刃 rèn sword

刀 + 、 = 刃

用"、"来指示刀"刃"的位置。指事字。

", " represents the edge of a knife.

| 刀 | 刃 | | | | | | | | 3 |
|---|---|---|---|---|---|---|---|---|---|
| 刃 | 刃 | 刃 | 刃 | 刃 | 刃 | 刃 | 刃 | 刃 | |

# 分 fēn to separate

八 + 刀 = 分

用"刀"子把东西切"分"开。会意字。

We use a knife to separate something.

| ノ | 八 | 分 | | | | | | | 4 |
|---|---|---|---|---|---|---|---|---|---|
| 分 | 分 | 分 | 分 | 分 | 分 | 分 | 分 | 分 | |

# 召 zhào to summon

刀 + 口 = 召

号"召"人要用"口"号。形声字，"刀"作声旁。

口 shows a mouth. Use one's mouth to call on people to do something. 刀 is the phonetic component.

| 刀 | 刁 | 召 | 召 | | | | | | 5 |
|---|---|---|---|---|---|---|---|---|---|
| 召 | 召 | 召 | 召 | 召 | 召 | 召 | 召 | 召 | |

# 剪 jiǎn scissors

前 + 刀 = 剪

"剪"子是用两把"刀"子构成的。形声字，"前"作声旁。

The scissors are composed of two knives. 前 is the phonetic component.

| 、 | 丷 | 丷 | 广 | 芦 | 芮 | 前 | 前 | 剪 | 11 |
|---|---|---|---|---|---|---|---|---|---|
| 剪 | 剪 | 剪 | 剪 | 剪 | 剪 | 剪 | 剪 | 剪 | 剪 |

# 【刂部】

"刂"是由"刀"字演变而来，刂部的字多和使用刀具有关。立刀旁的位置在字的右侧。

刂 is evolved from 刀. Characters with the radical 刂 refer mostly to the use of a knife. It is placed on the right side.

刂

称说：立刀旁

Name: lìdāopáng                standing knife

刀 → 刂

**笔顺及笔画数** Stroke order and number

| ㇆ | 刂 | | | 2 |
|---|---|---|---|---|

| 刂 | 刂 | 刂 | 刂 | 刂 |
|---|---|---|---|---|

---

利    lì    sharp

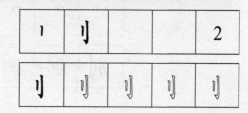

禾 + 刂 = 利

"禾"表示庄稼，割庄稼的"刀"子是锋"利"的。会意字。

禾 shows the stalk of a crop. 刂 shows a knife. The knives used for cutting crops are very sharp.

| ㇒ | 二 | 千 | 禾 | 禾 | 利 | | 7 |
|---|---|---|---|---|---|---|---|

| 利 | 利 | 利 | 利 | 利 | 利 | 利 | 利 | 利 |
|---|---|---|---|---|---|---|---|---|

---

删    shān    to delete

册 + 刂 = 删

古代"册"字表示用竹简作成的书，把竹简上的字"删"去要用"刀"子。会意字。

册 looks like bamboo slips tied together, and 刂 represents a knife. In ancient China a knife was used to delete characters.

| ㇒ | 刀 | 刑 | 刑 | 册 | 删 | 7 |
|---|---|---|---|---|---|---|

| 删 | 删 | 删 | 删 | 删 | 删 | 删 | 删 |
|---|---|---|---|---|---|---|---|

**刻** kè to carve

亥 + 刂 = 刻

用"刀"子进行雕"刻"。形声字。
We use a knife to carve something.

| 、 | 二 | 亠 | 亥 | 亥 | 亥 | 刻 | | 8 |

| 刻 | 刻 | 刻 | 刻 | 刻 | 刻 | 刻 | 刻 | 刻 |

**别** bié to leave

另 + 刂 = 别

分"别"就像用"刀"子把东西分开一样。
Leaving each other looks like the separation of something by using a knife.

| ' | 口 | 口 | 号 | 另 | 别 | | | 7 |

| 别 | 别 | 别 | 别 | 别 | 别 | 别 | 别 | 别 |

**到** dào to arrive

至 + 刂 = 到

"至"有"到"的意思。形声字，"刂"作声旁。
至 means "to arrive". 刂 is the phonetic component.

| 一 | 工 | 五 | 至 | 至 | 至 | 到 | | 8 |

| 到 | 到 | 到 | 到 | 到 | 到 | 到 | 到 | 到 |

**刚** gāng firm

冈 + 刂 = 刚

"刚"强的性格就像钢"刀"一样。"冈"作声旁。
A person's character is as firm as a knife. 冈 is the phonetic component.

| 丨 | 冂 | 刀 | 冈 | 刚 | | | | 6 |

| 刚 | 刚 | 刚 | 刚 | 刚 | 刚 | 刚 | 刚 | 刚 |

# 【力部】

力　　　lì　　　　　　　　　　strength, force

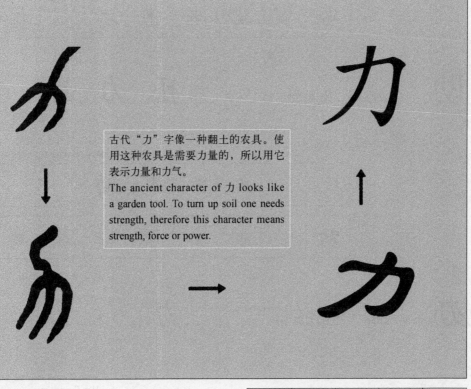

古代"力"字像一种翻土的农具。使用这种农具是需要力量的，所以用它表示力量和力气。
The ancient character of 力 looks like a garden tool. To turn up soil one needs strength, therefore this character means strength, force or power.

| フ | 力 | | | 2 |
|---|---|---|---|---|
| 力 | 力 | 力 | 力 | 力 |

动　　dòng　　to move　　　云 + 力 = 动　

运"动"是需要"力"量的。
A movement requires force.

| 一 | 二 | 云 | 云 | 动 | | | 6 |
|---|---|---|---|---|---|---|---|
| 动 | 动 | 动 | 动 | 动 | 动 | 动 | 动 | 动 |

17

劣　liè　bad

少 + 力 = 劣

干活时出"力""少"，被认为是不好的。
少 means few. Working without exerting oneself is regarded as bad.

| 丿 | 八 | 小 | 少 | 劣 | | | 6 |

| 劣 | 劣 | 劣 | 劣 | 劣 | 劣 | 劣 | 劣 | 劣 |

助　zhù　to help

且 + 力 = 助

帮"助"别人是要付出"力"气的。
Helping someone requires the use of one's power.

| 丨 | 冂 | 月 | 月 | 且 | 助 | | 7 |

| 助 | 助 | 助 | 助 | 助 | 助 | 助 | 助 | 助 |

办　bàn　to handle

力 + 八 = 办

"办"事情是要付出"力"气的。
Handling something requires force.

| 力 | 办 | 办 | | | | 4 |

| 办 | 办 | 办 | 办 | 办 | 办 | 办 | 办 | 办 |

勇　yǒng　brave

甬 + 力 = 勇

"力"气大的人常常很"勇"敢。"甬"作声旁。
One with great strength is often brave. 甬 is the phonetic component.

| 丶 | 乛 | 厂 | 丙 | 丙 | 甬 | 甬 | 勇 | 9 |

| 勇 | 勇 | 勇 | 勇 | 勇 | 勇 | 勇 | 勇 | 勇 |

# 【儿部】

"儿"部的字有些与人有关。儿字旁的位置一般在字的下部。
Some characters with the radical 儿 are relevant to human beings.
It is usually placed at the bottom.

儿 [兒] ér          son, child

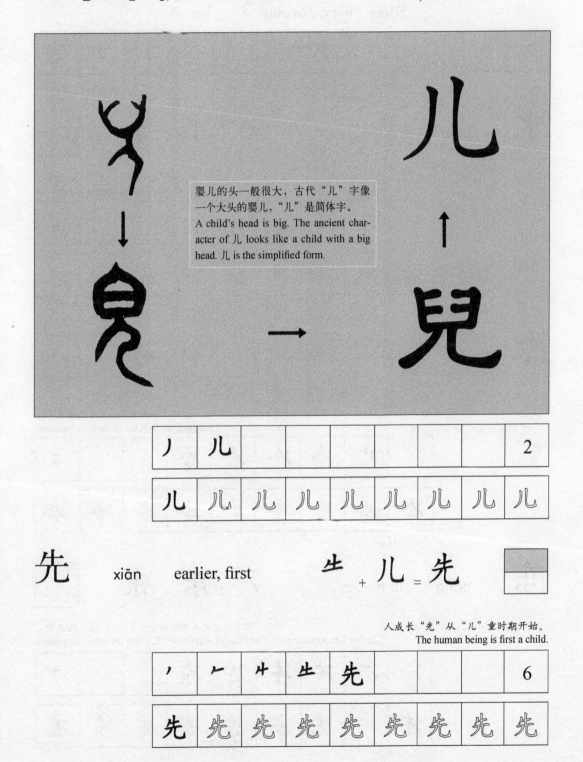

婴儿的头一般很大，古代"儿"字像一个大头的婴儿，"儿"是简体字。
A child's head is big. The ancient character of 儿 looks like a child with a big head. 儿 is the simplified form.

| ノ | 儿 | | | | | | | 2 |
|---|---|---|---|---|---|---|---|---|
| 儿 | 儿 | 儿 | 儿 | 儿 | 儿 | 儿 | 儿 | 儿 |

先    xiān    earlier, first      生 + 儿 = 先

人成长"先"从"儿"童时期开始。
The human being is first a child.

| ノ | 一 | 屮 | 生 | 先 | | | | 6 |
|---|---|---|---|---|---|---|---|---|
| 先 | 先 | 先 | 先 | 先 | 先 | 先 | 先 | 先 |

19

# 【冫部】

> "冫"部的字多和寒冷有关。两点水旁在字的左侧。
> Characters with the radical 冫 refer to being cold. It is placed on the left side.

冫    称说：两点水
     Name: liǎngdiǎnshuǐ      ice

| 丶 | 冫 |
|---|---|

| 冫 | 冫 | 冫 | 冫 | 冫 | 冫 | 2 |
|---|---|---|---|---|---|---|

## 冰　bīng　ice

冫 + 水 = 冰

"水"遇"冷"结成"冰"。会意字。
水 means water. Frozen water turns into ice.

| 冫 | 冫 | 冫 | 冰 | 冰 | | | 6 |
|---|---|---|---|---|---|---|---|

| 冰 | 冰 | 冰 | 冰 | 冰 | 冰 | 冰 | 冰 | 冰 |
|---|---|---|---|---|---|---|---|---|

## 冷　lěng　cold

冫 + 令 = 冷

"冫"表示寒冷。"令"作声旁。
冫 means cold. 令 is the phonetic component.

| 冫 | 冫 | 冹 | 冹 | 冷 | 冷 | | 7 |
|---|---|---|---|---|---|---|---|

| 冷 | 冷 | 冷 | 冷 | 冷 | 冷 | 冷 | 冷 | 冷 |
|---|---|---|---|---|---|---|---|---|

## 冻　dòng　to freeze

由于"寒冷"才使人或东西受"冻"。"东"作声旁。
In low temperature people and things will freeze. 东 is the phonetic component.

| 冫 | 冫 | 冸 | 冻 | 冻 | 冻 | | 7 |
|---|---|---|---|---|---|---|---|

| 冻 | 冻 | 冻 | 冻 | 冻 | 冻 | 冻 | 冻 | 冻 |
|---|---|---|---|---|---|---|---|---|

# 【又部】

又　　　yòu　　　　　　　　　　　　　　right hand

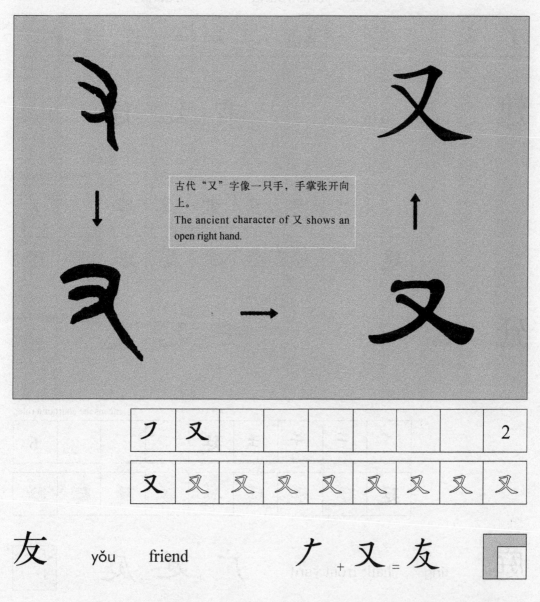

古代"又"字像一只手，手掌张开向上。
The ancient character of 又 shows an open right hand.

| フ | 又 | | | | | | | 2 |
|---|---|---|---|---|---|---|---|---|
| 又 | 又 | 又 | 又 | 又 | 又 | 又 | 又 | 又 |

友　　yǒu　　friend　　　　　ナ ＋ 又 ＝ 友

"ナ"表示一只手，"又"表示另一只手，两手相握表示"友"好。
ナ indicates a hand. 又 shows another hand. Two people holding hands is a sign of friendship between them.

| 一 | ナ | 友 | | | | | | 4 |
|---|---|---|---|---|---|---|---|---|
| 友 | 友 | 友 | 友 | 友 | 友 | 友 | 友 | 友 |

21

# 【廴部】

廴部的字有的和建筑有关。廴的位置在左下侧。
Some characters with the radical 廴 refer to buildings. It is placed on the left side.

廴　　　称说：建之旁
　　　　Name: jiànzhīpáng　　　structure

| 廴 | 廴 | 廴 | 廴 | 廴 | 廴 | 2 |

建　jiàn　to build　　　聿 + 廴 = 建

"建"是个合体字，"廴"表义。
建 is a compound character. 廴 indicates "to build".

| ⁊ | ⁊ | ⁊ | ⁊ | ⁊ | 聿 | 建 | 8 |
| 建 | 建 | 建 | 建 | 建 | 建 | 建 | 建 | 建 |

廷　tíng　court　　　壬 + 廴 = 廷

宫"廷"是豪华的建筑。
廷 means the court of a ruler.

| 一 | 二 | 千 | 壬 | 廷 | | 6 |
| 廷 | 廷 | 廷 | 廷 | 廷 | 廷 | 廷 | 廷 | 廷 |

庭　tíng　hall; front yard　　　广 + 廷 = 庭

"广"表示宽广。"庭"院是宽敞的地方。"廷"作声旁。
广 means vast. 庭, the front yard, is open and spacious. 廷 is the phonetic component.

| 丶 | 二 | 广 | 广 | 庄 | 庄 | 庄 | 庭 | 9 |
| 庭 | 庭 | 庭 | 庭 | 庭 | 庭 | 庭 | 庭 | 庭 |

# 【厂部】

"厂" 部的字有的和房间一类的东西有关。厂字旁的位置很固定。
Some characters with the radical 厂 refer to houses. Its position is fixed.

厂 [廠]　chǎng　factory, yard

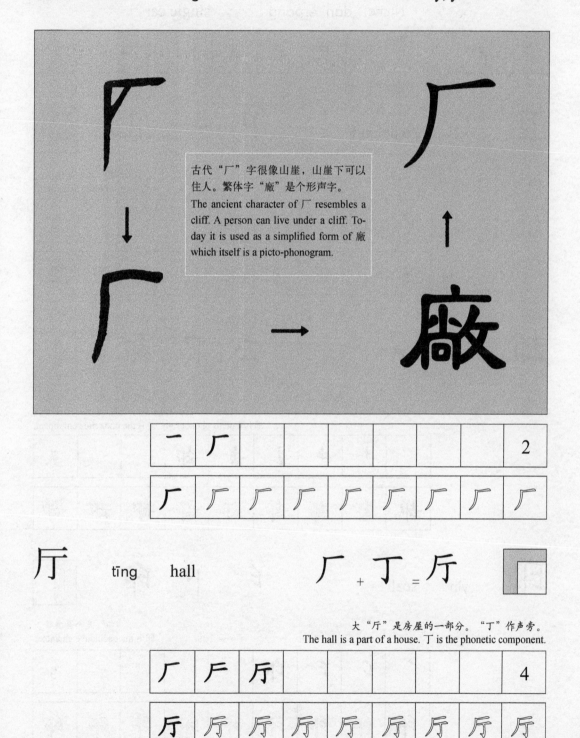

古代 "厂" 字很像山崖，山崖下可以住人。繁体字 "廠" 是个形声字。
The ancient character of 厂 resembles a cliff. A person can live under a cliff. Today it is used as a simplified form of 廠 which itself is a picto-phonogram.

| 一 | 厂 | | | | | | | | 2 |
|---|---|---|---|---|---|---|---|---|---|
| 厂 | 厂 | 厂 | 厂 | 厂 | 厂 | 厂 | 厂 | 厂 | 厂 |

厅　tīng　hall

厂 + 丁 = 厅

大 "厅" 是房屋的一部分。"丁" 作声旁。
The hall is a part of a house. 丁 is the phonetic component.

| 厂 | 厅 | 厅 | | | | | | | 4 |
|---|---|---|---|---|---|---|---|---|---|
| 厅 | 厅 | 厅 | 厅 | 厅 | 厅 | 厅 | 厅 | 厅 | 厅 |

23

# 【卩部】

卩部的字许多都是简体字，卩充当一个符号，卩的位置多在右侧。

Many characters with the radical 卩 are simplified, and 卩 is a sign placed mostly on the right side.

卩    称说：单耳旁

Name:  dān' ěrpáng    single ear

| ⺋ | 卩 | | | 卩 | 卩 | 卩 | 卩 | 卩 | 卩 | 2 |

---

卫    wèi    to defend

卩 + 一 = 卫

"卫"是个简体字。
卫 is a simplified character.

| 卩 | 卫 | | | | | | | | | 3 |
| 卫 | 卫 | 卫 | 卫 | 卫 | 卫 | 卫 | 卫 | 卫 | | |

---

却    què    yet

去 + 卩 = 却

"却"是个形声字。"去"作声旁。
却 is a picto-phonogram. 去 is the phonetic component.

| 一 | 十 | 土 | 去 | 去 | 却 | | | | | 7 |
| 却 | 却 | 却 | 却 | 却 | 却 | 却 | 却 | 却 | | |

---

印    yìn    seal

⺒ + 卩 = 印

"印"是个会意字。
印 is an associative character.

| ⺀ | ⺄ | ⺒ | 印 | | | | | | | 5 |
| 印 | 印 | 印 | 印 | 印 | 印 | 印 | 印 | 印 | | |

# 【阝部】

阝部的字分两种。阝在左侧的字多和山坡、地势有关。阝在右侧的字多和城邑、区域有关。

Characters with the radical 阝 are of two types. 阝 on the left side refers to a hill or terrain, and on the right refers to a city or an area.

阝

称说：耳刀旁

Name: ěrdāopáng　　　　　　mound, town

| 𠃌 | 阝 |
|---|---|

| 阝 | 阝 | 阝 | 阝 | 阝 | 阝 | 2 |
|---|---|---|---|---|---|---|

## 阳　yáng　sun

阝 + 日 = 阳

"阝"表示山坡，"日"表示太阳。山有阳光的那面为"阳"面。

阝 means hill. 日 means sun. The two together show the sunny side of a mountain.

| 阝 | 阝l | 阳l | 阳 | 阳 | | 6 |
|---|---|---|---|---|---|---|

| 阳 | 阳 | 阳 | 阳 | 阳 | 阳 | 阳 | 阳 | 阳 |
|---|---|---|---|---|---|---|---|---|

## 阴　yīn　overcast

阝 + 月 = 阴

"阝"表示山坡，"月"表示月亮。山背"阴"的地方就像月光下一样阴暗。

阝 means hill. 月 means the moon. At the side of a hill where the sun can't reach, it's as dark as in the moonlight.

| 阝 | 阝月 | 阴 | 阴 | 阴 | | 6 |
|---|---|---|---|---|---|---|

| 阴 | 阴 | 阴 | 阴 | 阴 | 阴 | 阴 | 阴 | 阴 |
|---|---|---|---|---|---|---|---|---|

## 院　yuàn　courtyard

阝 + 完 = 院

"院"子是地势平坦的地方。"完"作声旁。

阝 shows terrain. A courtyard is on flat terrain. 完 is the phonetic component.

| 阝 | 阝` | 阝` | 阝 | 阝 | 陀 | 院 | 9 |
|---|---|---|---|---|---|---|---|

| 院 | 院 | 院 | 院 | 院 | 院 | 院 | 院 | 院 |
|---|---|---|---|---|---|---|---|---|

# 都 dū capital

者 + 阝 = 都

首 "都" 是座城市。
阝 shows a city. A capital is a city.

| 一 | 十 | 土 | 耂 | 耂 | 者 | 者 | 者 | 都 | 10 |
|---|---|---|---|---|---|---|---|---|---|
| 都 | 都 | 都 | 都 | 都 | 都 | 都 | 都 | 都 | 都 |

# 部 bù part, unit

立 + 口 + 阝 = 部

"地区" 是某个地方的一 "部" 分。
阝 shows an area. A unit is part of an area.

| 、 | 丶 | 亠 | 立 | 立 | 产 | 音 | 音 | 部 | 10 |
|---|---|---|---|---|---|---|---|---|---|
| 部 | 部 | 部 | 部 | 部 | 部 | 部 | 部 | 部 | 部 |

# 那 nà that

刅 + 阝 = 那

"那" 指示某个地方。
阝 shows a place. 那 demonstrates a certain place.

| 刁 | 刁 | 刅 | 刅 | 那 | | | | | 6 |
|---|---|---|---|---|---|---|---|---|---|
| 那 | 那 | 那 | 那 | 那 | 那 | 那 | 那 | 那 | |

# 邻 lín neighbour

令 + 阝 = 邻

居住在你旁边的人家为 "邻" 居。"令" 作声旁。
阝 shows a place. A neighbour is a person living near you. 令 is the phonetic component.

| 丿 | 人 | 卆 | 今 | 令 | 邻 | | | | 7 |
|---|---|---|---|---|---|---|---|---|---|
| 邻 | 邻 | 邻 | 邻 | 邻 | 邻 | 邻 | 邻 | 邻 | |

# 【大部】

大     dà                   big

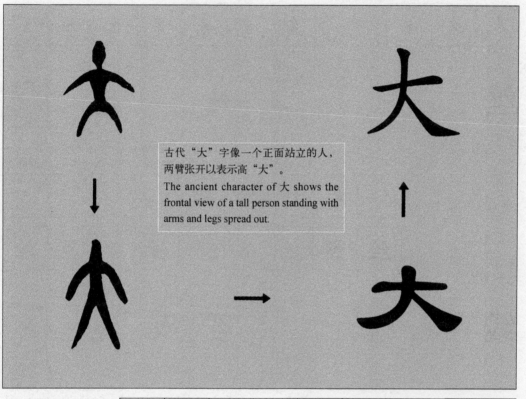

古代“大”字像一个正面站立的人，两臂张开以表示高“大”。
The ancient character of 大 shows the frontal view of a tall person standing with arms and legs spread out.

| 一 | 丁 | 大 | | | | | | 3 |
|---|---|---|---|---|---|---|---|---|
| 大 | 大 | 大 | 大 | 大 | 大 | 大 | 大 | 大 |

天    tiān   sky         一 + 大 = 天

古代“大”字是一站立的人，头上加一横指示头顶之上是“天”空。
天 shows a person standing with a horizontal stroke on his head to indicate what is above his head, the sky.

| 一 | 天 | | | | | | | 4 |
|---|---|---|---|---|---|---|---|---|
| 天 | 天 | 天 | 天 | 天 | 天 | 天 | 天 | 天 |

27

# 【纟部】

纟部的字许多和丝线有关。绞丝旁的位置在字的左侧。
Characters with the radical 纟 relate to silk and thread. It is placed on the left side.

纟　　　　　称说：绞丝旁
　　　　　　Name: jiǎosīpáng　　　silk

| ↅ | 纟 | 纟 |
| --- | --- | --- |

| 纟 | 纟 | 纟 | 纟 | 纟 | 纟 | 3 |
| --- | --- | --- | --- | --- | --- | --- |

丝　　sī　silk

丝 + 一 = 丝

古代"丝"字像一缕丝线。纟是"丝"字的一半。
The ancient character of 丝 depicts twisted silken threads. 纟 is half of 丝.

| ↅ | 纟 | 纟 | 丝 | 丝 | | | | 5 |
| --- | --- | --- | --- | --- | --- | --- | --- | --- |

| 丝 | 丝 | 丝 | 丝 | 丝 | 丝 | 丝 | 丝 | 丝 |
| --- | --- | --- | --- | --- | --- | --- | --- | --- |

线　　xiàn　thread

纟 + 戋 = 线

"纟"表示丝线。"戋"作声旁。
纟 shows thread. 戋 is the phonetic component.

| 纟 | 纟 | 纟 | 纩 | 线 | 线 | | 8 |
| --- | --- | --- | --- | --- | --- | --- | --- |

| 线 | 线 | 线 | 线 | 线 | 线 | 线 | 线 | 线 |
| --- | --- | --- | --- | --- | --- | --- | --- | --- |

结　　jié　knot

纟 + 吉 = 结

"线绳"可以打"结"。"吉"作声旁。
We can use thread to tie a knot. 吉 is the phonetic component.

| 纟 | 纟 | 纩 | 纩 | 纩 | 结 | 结 | | 9 |
| --- | --- | --- | --- | --- | --- | --- | --- | --- |

| 结 | 结 | 结 | 结 | 结 | 结 | 结 | 结 | 结 |
| --- | --- | --- | --- | --- | --- | --- | --- | --- |

# 【工部】

工部的字有的和工作有关，有的"工"作声旁。工字旁的位置较灵活。

Some characters with the radical 工 relate to work. Sometimes 工 is the phonetic component. Its position is flexible.

工 　　　　gōng 　　　　　　　　　　work

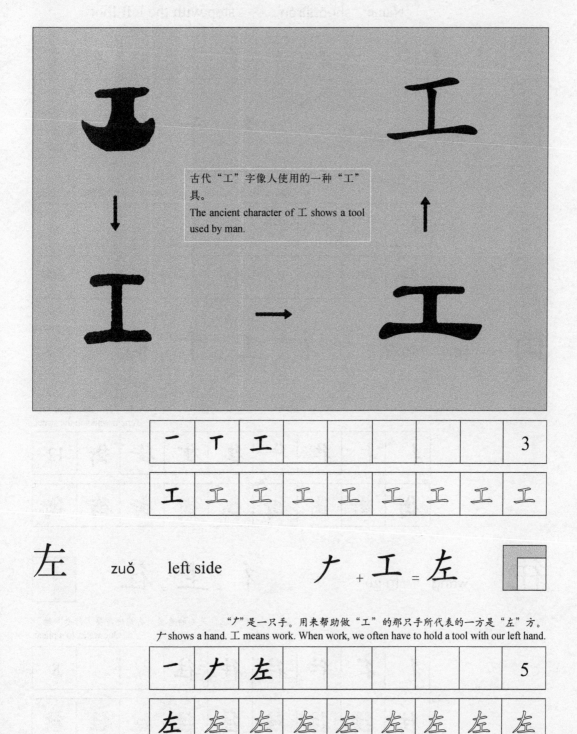

古代"工"字像人使用的一种"工"具。

The ancient character of 工 shows a tool used by man.

| 一 | 丁 | 工 | | | | | | 3 |
|---|---|---|---|---|---|---|---|---|

| 工 | 工 | 工 | 工 | 工 | 工 | 工 | 工 | 工 |
|---|---|---|---|---|---|---|---|---|

左 　　zuǒ　　left side 　　　　ナ ＋ 工 ＝ 左

"ナ"是一只手。用来帮助做"工"的那只手所代表的一方是"左"方。

ナ shows a hand. 工 means work. When work, we often have to hold a tool with our left hand.

| 一 | ナ | 左 | | | | | | 5 |
|---|---|---|---|---|---|---|---|---|

| 左 | 左 | 左 | 左 | 左 | 左 | 左 | 左 | 左 |
|---|---|---|---|---|---|---|---|---|

29

# 【彳部】

彳　　称说：双立人

Name: shuānlìrén　　step with the left foot

| ヽ | ク | 彳 |
|---|---|---|

| 彳 | 彳 | 彳 | 彳 | 彳 | 彳 | 3 |
|---|---|---|---|---|---|---|

行　xíng　to walk　　彳 + 丁 = 行

古代"行"字像一个通往四方的十字路口。
The ancient 行 resembles a crossroads going in four directions.

| 彳 | 彳 | 彳 | 行 | | | | | 6 |
|---|---|---|---|---|---|---|---|---|

| 行 | 行 | 行 | 行 | 行 | 行 | 行 | 行 | 行 |
|---|---|---|---|---|---|---|---|---|

街　jiē　street　　彳 + 圭 + 丁 = 街

人在"街"上"行走"。
A man walks in the street.

| 彳 | 彳 | 彳 | 彳 | 往 | 往 | 往 | 街 | 12 |
|---|---|---|---|---|---|---|---|---|

| 街 | 街 | 街 | 街 | 街 | 街 | 街 | 街 | 街 |
|---|---|---|---|---|---|---|---|---|

往　wǎng　to go　　彳 + 主 = 往

"往"是去的意思。去某地是要"行走"的。
One walks to a place.

| 彳 | 彳 | 彳 | 彳 | 往 | 往 | | | 8 |
|---|---|---|---|---|---|---|---|---|

| 往 | 往 | 往 | 往 | 往 | 往 | 往 | 往 | 往 |
|---|---|---|---|---|---|---|---|---|

# 【子部】

子　　　　zǐ　　　　　　　　　　son, child

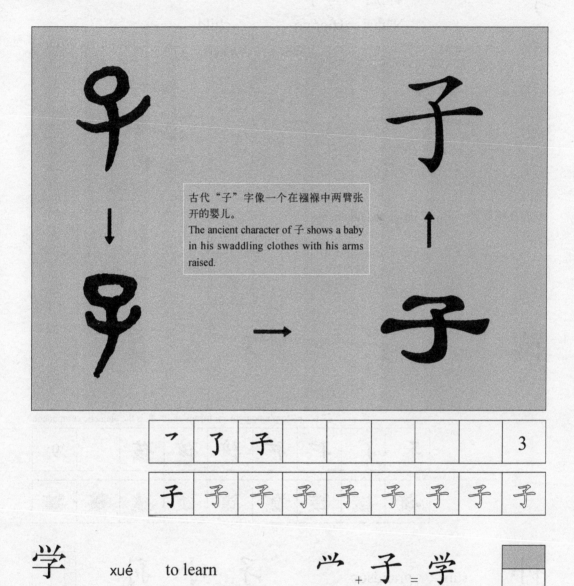

古代"子"字像一个在襁褓中两臂张开的婴儿。
The ancient character of 子 shows a baby in his swaddling clothes with his arms raised.

| ㇇ | 了 | 子 | | | | | | 3 |
|---|---|---|---|---|---|---|---|---|
| 子 | 子 | 子 | 子 | 子 | 子 | 子 | 子 | 子 |

学　　　xué　　to learn　　　　　丷 + 子 = 学

"子"表示孩子。孩"子"要上"学"。
子 shows a child. Children should go to school for learning.

| 丶 | 丷 | 丷 | 丷 | 兴 | 学 | | | 8 |
|---|---|---|---|---|---|---|---|---|
| 学 | 学 | 学 | 学 | 学 | 学 | 学 | 学 | 学 |

31

# 【子部】

子

称说：子字旁

Name: zǐzìpáng　　　child

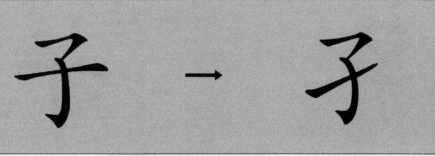

**笔顺及笔画数** Stroke order and number

| フ | 了 | 子 | | 3 |
|---|---|---|---|---|

| 子 | 孑 | 孑 | 孑 | 孑 |
|---|---|---|---|---|

---

孩　　hái　　child

子 + 亥 = 孩

"子"表示孩子。形声字，"亥"是声旁。
孩 is a picto-phonogram. 子 means child. 亥 is the phonetic component.

| 子 | 孑 | 疒 | 孒 | 珓 | 孩 | 孩 | | 9 |
|---|---|---|---|---|---|---|---|---|

| 孩 | 孩 | 孩 | 孩 | 孩 | 孩 | 孩 | 孩 | 孩 |
|---|---|---|---|---|---|---|---|---|

---

孙　　sūn　　grandson

子 + 小 = 孙

在家庭中排行最"小"的孩"子"是"孙"子。
子 means child. 小 means young. The grandson is the youngest in the family.

| 子 | 引 | 孑 | 孙 | | | | 6 |
|---|---|---|---|---|---|---|---|

| 孙 | 孙 | 孙 | 孙 | 孙 | 孙 | 孙 | 孙 | 孙 |
|---|---|---|---|---|---|---|---|---|

# 【口部】

口部的字和口腔的动作有关。口字旁多在字的左侧。
Characters with the radical 口 are relevant to mouth. It is mostly placed on the left side.

口    kǒu    mouth

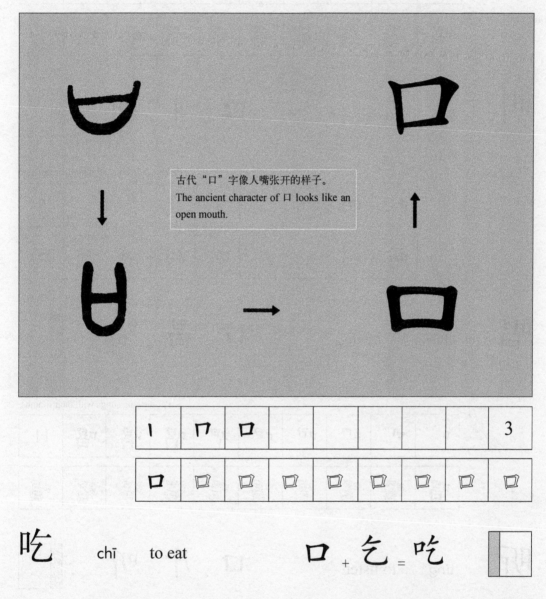

古代"口"字像人嘴张开的样子。
The ancient character of 口 looks like an open mouth.

| 丨 | 冂 | 口 | | | | | | | 3 |
|---|---|---|---|---|---|---|---|---|---|

| 口 | 口 | 口 | 口 | 口 | 口 | 口 | 口 | 口 | 口 |
|---|---|---|---|---|---|---|---|---|---|

吃    chī    to eat         口 + 乞 = 吃

用"口"来"吃"东西。"乞"作声旁。
People use their mouths to eat. 乞 is the phonetic component.

| 口 | 口ノ | 吃 | 吃 | | | | | | 6 |
|---|---|---|---|---|---|---|---|---|---|

| 吃 | 吃 | 吃 | 吃 | 吃 | 吃 | 吃 | 吃 | 吃 |
|---|---|---|---|---|---|---|---|---|

33

**喝**    hē    to drink      口 + 曷 = 喝

用"口"来"喝"水。"曷"作声旁。
People drink with their mouths. 曷 is the phonetic component.

| 口 | 口ˋ | 口冂 | 口冎 | 口日 | 口日 | 喝 | 喝 | 喝 | 12 |
|---|---|---|---|---|---|---|---|---|---|
| 喝 | 喝 | 喝 | 喝 | 喝 | 喝 | 喝 | 喝 | 喝 | 喝 |

**叫**    jiào    to call      口 + 丩 = 叫

用"口"来呼"叫"。
People call someone with their mouths.

| 口 | 叫 | 叫 | | | | | | | 5 |
|---|---|---|---|---|---|---|---|---|---|
| 叫 | 叫 | 叫 | 叫 | 叫 | 叫 | 叫 | 叫 | 叫 | |

**唱**    chàng    to sing      口 + 昌 = 唱

用"口"来"唱"歌。
People sing songs with their mouths.

| 口 | 口ˊ | 口冂 | 口冎 | 口日 | 唱 | 唱 | 唱 | 唱 | 11 |
|---|---|---|---|---|---|---|---|---|---|
| 唱 | 唱 | 唱 | 唱 | 唱 | 唱 | 唱 | 唱 | 唱 | 唱 |

**听**    tīng    to listen      口 + 斤 = 听

"口"说的话可以"听"到。
People listen to spoken words.

| 口 | 口ˊ | 听 | 听 | 听 | | | | | 7 |
|---|---|---|---|---|---|---|---|---|---|
| 听 | 听 | 听 | 听 | 听 | 听 | 听 | 听 | 听 | |

34

# 【山部】

山部的字多和山有关。山字旁的位置较灵活。
Most characters with the radical 山 refer to mountain. Its position is flexible.

山　　　　　shān　　　　　　　　　　　hill, mountain

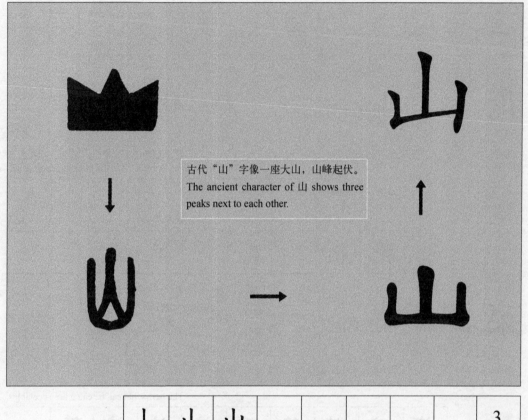

古代"山"字像一座大山，山峰起伏。
The ancient character of 山 shows three peaks next to each other.

| l | 凵 | 山 | | | | | | 3 |
|---|---|---|---|---|---|---|---|---|
| 山 | 山 | 山 | 山 | 山 | 山 | 山 | 山 | 山 |

岭　　　lǐng　　ridge　　　　　山 + 令 = 岭　　

"岭"是"山"的一部分。"令"作声旁。
岭 means ridge. A ridge is part of a mountain. 令 is the phonetic component.

| 山 | 山 | 屿 | 屿 | 岭 | 岭 | | | 8 |
|---|---|---|---|---|---|---|---|---|
| 岭 | 岭 | 岭 | 岭 | 岭 | 岭 | 岭 | 岭 | 岭 |

# 【艹部】

艹部的字多和草木植物有关。草字头在字的上部。
Characters with the radical 艹 relate mostly to herbs and plants. 艹 is placed at the top.

艹　　　称说：草字头
　　　Name: cǎozìtóu　　　　　　　　grass

| 一 | 十 | 艹 |
|---|---|---|

| 艹 | 艹 | 艹 | 艹 | 艹 | 艹 | 3 |
|---|---|---|---|---|---|---|

花　huā　flower　　　　　艹 + 化 = 花　

草木植物多开"花"。"化"作声旁。
Most herbs have flowers. 化 is the phonetic component.

| 艹 | 艹 | 艹 | 花 | | | 7 |
|---|---|---|---|---|---|---|

| 花 | 花 | 花 | 花 | 花 | 花 | 花 | 花 | 花 |
|---|---|---|---|---|---|---|---|---|

菜　cài　vegetable　　　　艹 + 采 = 菜　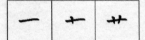

可以"采摘"食用的"草"称为"菜"。
The herbs that can be eaten are vegetables.

| 艹 | 艹 | 艹 | 艹 | 苎 | 苎 | 苹 | 苹 | 菜 | 11 |
|---|---|---|---|---|---|---|---|---|---|

| 菜 | 菜 | 菜 | 菜 | 菜 | 菜 | 菜 | 菜 | 菜 | 菜 |
|---|---|---|---|---|---|---|---|---|---|

茶　chá　tea　　　　艹 + 人 + 木 = 茶　

"茶"叶的形状像草一样。
Tea leaf resembles herb.

| 艹 | 艾 | 芩 | 芩 | 茶 | 茶 | 9 |
|---|---|---|---|---|---|---|

| 茶 | 茶 | 茶 | 茶 | 茶 | 茶 | 茶 | 茶 | 茶 |
|---|---|---|---|---|---|---|---|---|

# 【小部】

小          xiǎo                    small

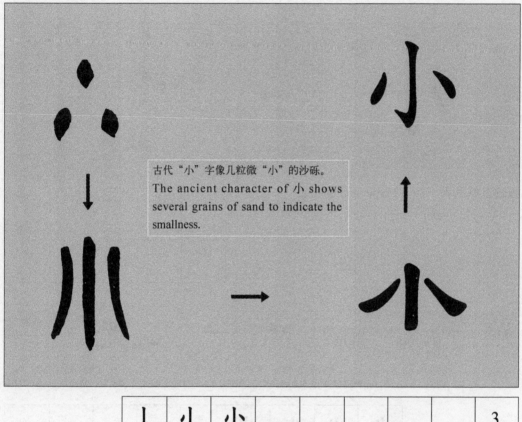

古代"小"字像几粒微"小"的沙砾。
The ancient character of 小 shows several grains of sand to indicate the smallness.

| 亅 | 小 | 小 | | | | | | 3 |
|---|---|---|---|---|---|---|---|---|
| 小 | 小 | 小 | 小 | 小 | 小 | 小 | 小 | 小 |

少          shǎo       few, little          小 + 丿 = 少

数量"小"就是不多的意思。
小 means small. A few means a small quantity.

| 小 | 少 | | | | | | | 4 |
|---|---|---|---|---|---|---|---|---|
| 少 | 少 | 少 | 少 | 少 | 少 | 少 | 少 | 少 |

# 【⺌部】

⺌是"小"的变体。⺌字旁成为一个符号，其位置在字的上部。
⺌ is a variant of 小. In the character with the radical ⺌, ⺌ is used as a sign. It is placed on the top.

小

称说：小字头

Name: xiǎozìtóu　　　　small

笔顺及笔画数　Stroke order and number

| 丨 | 丬 | 业 | | 3 |
|---|---|---|---|---|

| 业 | 业 | 业 | 业 | 业 |
|---|---|---|---|---|

光　guāng　light　　⺌ + 一 + 儿 = 光

古代字中"光"像一个人头上举着"火"把。"火"给人带来"光"明。
儿 shows a man. ⺌ shows fire. 光 shows a man lifting a torch. The fire gives light to people.

| 业 | 业 | 光 | 光 | | | | 6 |
|---|---|---|---|---|---|---|---|

| 光 | 光 | 光 | 光 | 光 | 光 | 光 | 光 | 光 |
|---|---|---|---|---|---|---|---|---|

常　cháng　often　　⺌ + 冖 + 吊 = 常

"常"是个合体字。
常 is a compound character.

| 业 | 业 | 业 | 常 | 常 | 常 | 常 | | 11 |
|---|---|---|---|---|---|---|---|---|

| 常 | 常 | 常 | 常 | 常 | 常 | 常 | 常 | 常 |
|---|---|---|---|---|---|---|---|---|

# 【土部】

土部的字多和土有关。土字旁在左侧时写法有点儿变形。
Most characters with the radical 土 refer to soil. When placed on the left side, 土 is written as 土.

土　　　　tǔ　　　　　　　　　　　　　soil

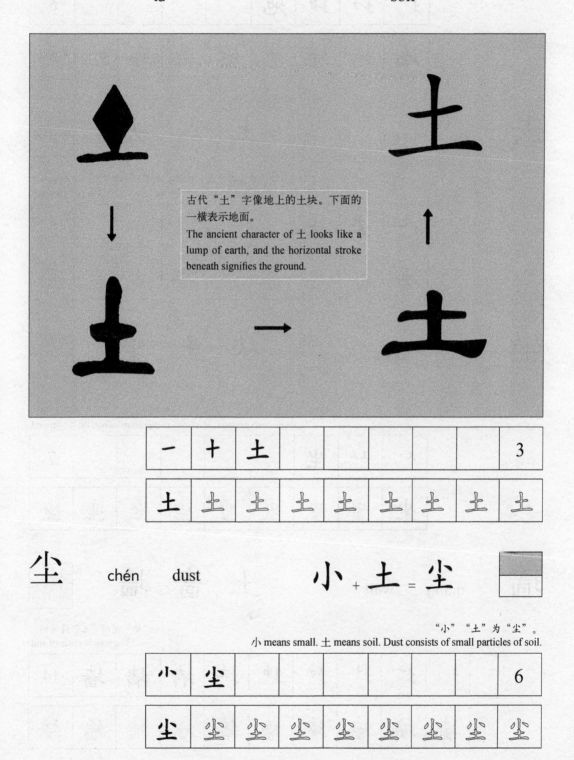

古代"土"字像地上的土块。下面的一横表示地面。
The ancient character of 土 looks like a lump of earth, and the horizontal stroke beneath signifies the ground.

| 一 | 十 | 土 |  |  |  |  |  | 3 |
|---|---|---|---|---|---|---|---|---|
| 土 | 土 | 土 | 土 | 土 | 土 | 土 | 土 | 土 |

尘　　chén　　dust　　　　　小 + 土 = 尘

"小""土"为"尘"。
小 means small. 土 means soil. Dust consists of small particles of soil.

| 小 | 尘 |  |  |  |  |  |  | 6 |
|---|---|---|---|---|---|---|---|---|
| 尘 | 尘 | 尘 | 尘 | 尘 | 尘 | 尘 | 尘 | 尘 |

39

地　　dì　　land　　　　　土 + 也 = 地

大 "地" 的成分是 "土"。
The element of land is soil.

| 土 | 圠 | 坲 | 地 | | | | | 6 |
|---|---|---|---|---|---|---|---|---|
| 地 | 地 | 地 | 地 | 地 | 地 | 地 | 地 | 地 |

去　　qù　　to go　　　　土 + 厶 = 去

路是由 "土" 修的。走路才可以 "去" 一个地方。
The road is made of soil. We walk on the road to go to a place.

| 土 | 去 | 去 | | | | | | 5 |
|---|---|---|---|---|---|---|---|---|
| 去 | 去 | 去 | 去 | 去 | 去 | 去 | 去 | 去 |

坐　　zuò　　to sit　　　　从 + 土 = 坐

两个 "人" "坐" 在土堆上。
从 shows two persons. 坐 shows two persons sitting on the ground.

| 人 | 从 | 坐 | | | | | | 7 |
|---|---|---|---|---|---|---|---|---|
| 坐 | 坐 | 坐 | 坐 | 坐 | 坐 | 坐 | 坐 | 坐 |

墙　　qiáng　　wall　　　　土 + 啬 = 墙

"墙" 是由 "土" 修筑的。
The wall is made of soil.

| 土 | 圠 | 圤 | 圤 | 坮 | 埮 | 培 | 墙 | 14 |
|---|---|---|---|---|---|---|---|---|
| 墙 | 墙 | 墙 | 墙 | 墙 | 墙 | 墙 | 墙 | 墙 |

# 【弓部】

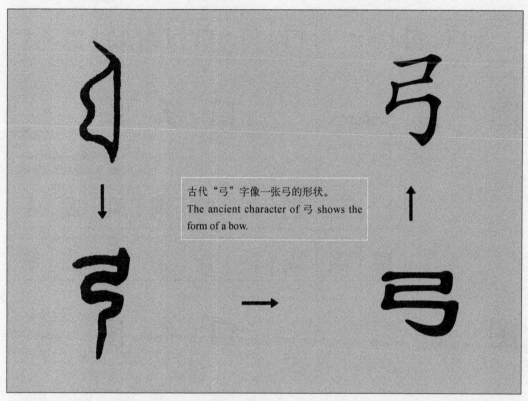

弓部的字多和弓箭有关。弓字旁一般在字的左侧。
Most characters with the radical 弓 relate to the bow and arrow. It is usually placed on the left side.

弓　　　　　gōng　　　　　　　　　bow

古代"弓"字像一张弓的形状。
The ancient character of 弓 shows the form of a bow.

| ㄱ | ㄱ | 弓 |  |  |  |  |  | 3 |
|---|---|---|---|---|---|---|---|---|
| 弓 | 弓 | 弓 | 弓 | 弓 | 弓 | 弓 | 弓 | 弓 |

张　　zhāng　　to draw　　　　弓 + 长 = 张

"弓"有"张"有"弛"。"长"作声旁。
A bow can be drawn and released. 长 is the phonetic component.

| 弓 | 弓´ | 弘 | 张 | 张 |  |  |  | 7 |
|---|---|---|---|---|---|---|---|---|
| 张 | 张 | 张 | 张 | 张 | 张 | 张 | 张 | 张 |

41

# 【口部】

口是一个方形的框框。口部的字都有一定的界限和范围。
口 resembles a square box. Characters with the radical 口 refer to limit and scope.

口

称说：大口框
Name: dàkǒukuàn    square

| 丨 | 冂 | 口 |
|---|---|---|

| 口 | 口 | 口 | 口 | 口 | 口 | 3 |
|---|---|---|---|---|---|---|

国    guó    country

口 + 玉 = 国

"国"家都有一定的疆界。
口 shows border. A country has borders.

| 丨 | 冂 | 冂 | 冃 | 用 | 国 | 国 | 国 | 8 |
|---|---|---|---|---|---|---|---|---|
| 国 | 国 | 国 | 国 | 国 | 国 | 国 | 国 | 国 |

图    tú    map

口 + 冬 = 图

地"图"一般是方形或长方形的。
口 shows scope. A map shows the scope of a place.

| 丨 | 冂 | 冂 | 图 | 图 | 图 | 图 | 图 | 8 |
|---|---|---|---|---|---|---|---|---|
| 图 | 图 | 图 | 图 | 图 | 图 | 图 | 图 | 图 |

园    yuán    garden

口 + 元 = 园

花"园"一般都有围墙。"元"作声旁。
口 shows limit. A garden has a limit (enclosure). 元 is the phonetic component.

| 丨 | 冂 | 冂 | 冃 | 园 | 园 | | 7 |
|---|---|---|---|---|---|---|---|
| 园 | 园 | 园 | 园 | 园 | 园 | 园 | 园 | 园 |

# 【巾部】

巾部的字多和巾一样的织物有关。巾字旁的位置较灵活。
Characters with the radical 巾 mostly refer to fabrics like a towel.
Its position is flexible.

巾　　　　　　jīn　　　　　　　　　　　　　　　towel

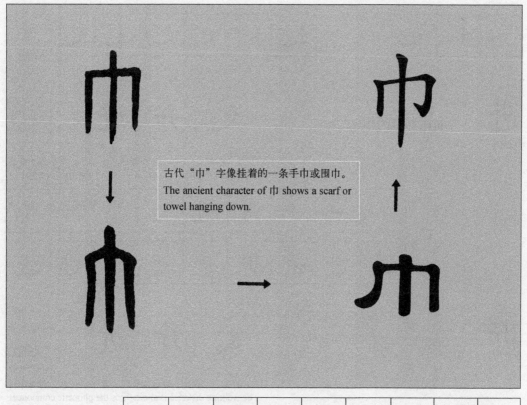

古代"巾"字像挂着的一条手巾或围巾。
The ancient character of 巾 shows a scarf or towel hanging down.

| 丶 | 冂 | 巾 | | | | | | | 3 |
|---|---|---|---|---|---|---|---|---|---|
| 巾 | 巾 | 巾 | 巾 | 巾 | 巾 | 巾 | 巾 | 巾 | |

布　　　bù　cloth　　　　　　　ナ ＋ 巾 ＝ 布

"ナ"表示一只手。"布"是手中拿着的像手"巾"一样的东西。
ナ shows a hand. The cloth is like a towel held in a hand.

| 一 | ナ | 布 | | | | | | | 5 |
|---|---|---|---|---|---|---|---|---|---|
| 布 | 布 | 布 | 布 | 布 | 布 | 布 | 布 | 布 | |

43

# 【辶部】

辶部的字多和行走有关。走之旁的位置很固定。
Characters with the radical 辶 relate mostly to walking. Its position is fixed.

辶　　称说：走之旁
　　　Name: zǒuzhīpáng　　　to walk

| 、 | 辶 | 辶 |
|---|---|---|

| 辶 | 辶 | 辶 | 辶 | 辶 | 辶 | 3 |
|---|---|---|---|---|---|---|

---

进　jìn　to enter　　　辶 + 井 = 进　

从外边"走"到里边叫"进"。"井"作声旁。
Walking from outside to inside is to enter. 井 is the phonetic component.

| 一 | 二 | 龶 | 井 | 进 | | | 7 |
|---|---|---|---|---|---|---|---|

| 进 | 进 | 进 | 进 | 进 | 进 | 进 | 进 | 进 |
|---|---|---|---|---|---|---|---|---|

---

近　jìn　near　　　辶 + 斤 = 近　

"走"的路程短叫"近"。"斤"作声旁。
The walking distance is short. 斤 is the phonetic component.

| ノ | 厂 | 斤 | 斤 | 近 | | | 7 |
|---|---|---|---|---|---|---|---|

| 近 | 近 | 近 | 近 | 近 | 近 | 近 | 近 | 近 |
|---|---|---|---|---|---|---|---|---|

---

远　yuǎn　far　　　辶 + 元 = 远　

"走"的路程长叫"远"。"元"作声旁。
The walking distance is long. 元 is the phonetic component.

| 一 | 二 | 元 | 远 | | | | 7 |
|---|---|---|---|---|---|---|---|

| 远 | 远 | 远 | 远 | 远 | 远 | 远 | 远 | 远 |
|---|---|---|---|---|---|---|---|---|

# 【马部】

马部的字多和马有关。马字旁一般在字的左侧。
Most characters with the radical 马 relate to the horse. It is placed on the left side.

## 马[馬]　mǎ　　　　　　　　　　　horse

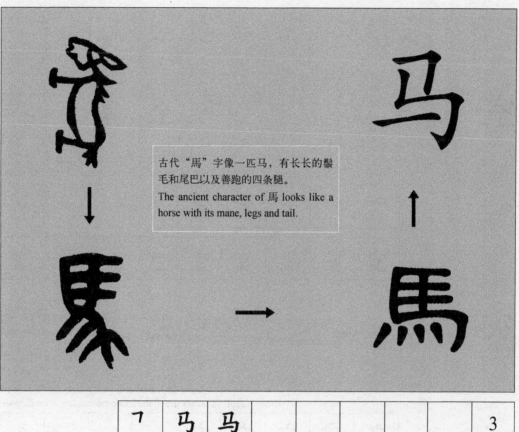

古代"馬"字像一匹马，有长长的鬃毛和尾巴以及善跑的四条腿。
The ancient character of 馬 looks like a horse with its mane, legs and tail.

| フ | 马 | 马 | | | | | | | 3 |
|---|---|---|---|---|---|---|---|---|---|
| 马 | 马 | 马 | 马 | 马 | 马 | 马 | 马 | 马 | |

## 骑　qí　to ride (an animal)　　马 + 奇 = 骑

人们把类似骑"马"的动作叫做"骑"。"奇"作声旁。
An action that resembles riding on a horse is called "to ride". 奇 is the phonetic component.

| 马 | 马′ | 驴 | 骑 | 骑 | | | | | 11 |
|---|---|---|---|---|---|---|---|---|---|
| 骑 | 骑 | 骑 | 骑 | 骑 | 骑 | 骑 | 骑 | 骑 | |

# 【宀部】

宀部的字多和房舍有关。宝盖头在字的上部。
Characters with the radical 宀 relate to house and room. It is placed at the top.

宀　　称说：宝盖头
　　　Name: bǎogàitóu　　roof

| 、 | 宀 | 宀 |
|---|---|---|

| 宀 | 宀 | 宀 | 宀 | 宀 | 宀 | 3 |
|---|---|---|---|---|---|---|

室　shì　room　　　宀 + 至 = 室

"至"是"到"的意思，到了房子里边就是"室"。
至 means to arrive, 宀 shows a roof. When we arrive at a house, we are in a room.

| 宀 | 宀 | 宀 | 宀 | 室 | | | | 9 |
|---|---|---|---|---|---|---|---|---|

| 室 | 室 | 室 | 室 | 室 | 室 | 室 | 室 | 室 |
|---|---|---|---|---|---|---|---|---|

灾　zāi　disaster　　　宀 + 火 = 灾

"宀"表示房间。房间里着"火"了是场"灾"难。
宀 shows a roof. 火 means fire. If the house catches fire, it's a disaster.

| 宀 | 宀 | 宀 | 灾 | 灾 | | | 7 |
|---|---|---|---|---|---|---|---|

| 灾 | 灾 | 灾 | 灾 | 灾 | 灾 | 灾 | 灾 | 灾 |
|---|---|---|---|---|---|---|---|---|

宿　sù　to lodge for the night　　　宀 + 佰 = 宿

"房子"可以住"宿"。
宀 shows a house. The house can be used to lodge for the night.

| 宀 | 宀 | 宀 | 宿 | 宿 | 宿 | 宿 | 宿 | 11 |
|---|---|---|---|---|---|---|---|---|

| 宿 | 宿 | 宿 | 宿 | 宿 | 宿 | 宿 | 宿 | 宿 |
|---|---|---|---|---|---|---|---|---|

# 【女部】

女部的字多和女性有关。女字旁多在字的左侧。
Most characters with the radical 女 relate to the female sex. It is placed on the left side.

女　　　nǚ　　　　　　　　　woman

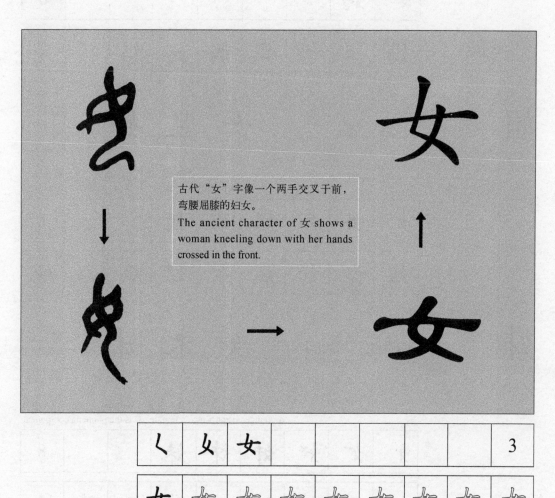

古代"女"字像一个两手交叉于前，弯腰屈膝的妇女。
The ancient character of 女 shows a woman kneeling down with her hands crossed in the front.

| く | 夂 | 女 | | | | | | 3 |
|---|---|---|---|---|---|---|---|---|
| 女 | 女 | 女 | 女 | 女 | 女 | 女 | 女 | 女 |

好　　hǎo　　good　　　　女 + 子 = 好

"女人"有了"孩子"是件"好"事。
子 means a child. 女 means woman. A woman bringing forth a child is good.

| 女 | 好 | | | | | | | 6 |
|---|---|---|---|---|---|---|---|---|
| 好 | 好 | 好 | 好 | 好 | 好 | 好 | 好 | 好 |

# 妈 mā mother

女 + 马 = 妈

"妈妈"是"女"性。"马"作声旁。
Mother is a female. 马 is the phonetic component.

| 女 | 妈 | | | | | | | 6 |
|---|---|---|---|---|---|---|---|---|
| 妈 | 妈 | 妈 | 妈 | 妈 | 妈 | 妈 | 妈 | 妈 |

# 姐 jiě elder sister

女 + 且 = 姐

"姐姐"是"女"性。"且"作声旁。
An elder sister is a female. 且 is the phonetic component.

| 女 | 刻 | 如 | 姐 | 姐 | 姐 | | | 8 |
|---|---|---|---|---|---|---|---|---|
| 姐 | 姐 | 姐 | 姐 | 姐 | 姐 | 姐 | 姐 | 姐 |

# 妹 mèi younger sister

女 + 未 = 妹

"妹妹"是"女"性。"未"作声旁。
A younger sister is also a female. 未 is the phonetic component.

| 女 | 女 | 女 | 妹 | 妹 | 妹 | | | 8 |
|---|---|---|---|---|---|---|---|---|
| 妹 | 妹 | 妹 | 妹 | 妹 | 妹 | 妹 | 妹 | 妹 |

# 妇 fù married woman

女 + 彐 = 妇

"彐"表示扫帚。一人"女"人手持扫帚扫地是"妇"女的形象。
彐 means broom. 妇 shows a woman sweeping the floor with a broom.

| 女 | 如 | 妇 | 妇 | | | | | 6 |
|---|---|---|---|---|---|---|---|---|
| 妇 | 妇 | 妇 | 妇 | 妇 | 妇 | 妇 | 妇 | 妇 |

# 【尸部】

尸部的字多和人或动物的躯体有关。尸字旁的位置较固定。
Most characters with the radical 尸 refer to the body of man or animal. Its position is fixed.

尸　　shī　　　　　　　　　　corpse

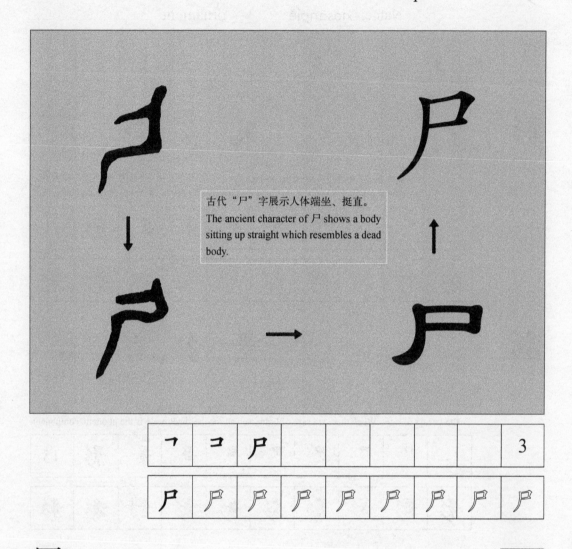

古代"尸"字展示人体端坐、挺直。
The ancient character of 尸 shows a body sitting up straight which resembles a dead body.

| ㇇ | コ | 尸 | | | | | | | 3 |
|---|---|---|---|---|---|---|---|---|---|
| 尸 | 尸 | 尸 | 尸 | 尸 | 尸 | 尸 | 尸 | 尸 | |

尾　　wěi　tail　　　　尸 + 毛 = 尾

"尸"表示动物的躯体。躯体后"毛"茸茸的东西是"尾"巴。
尸 shows the body of an animal. 毛 means hair. The animal's tail is found at the back of its body.

| 尸 | 尸 | 尸 | 屋 | 尾 | | | | | 7 |
|---|---|---|---|---|---|---|---|---|---|
| 尾 | 尾 | 尾 | 尾 | 尾 | 尾 | 尾 | 尾 | 尾 | |

# 【彡部】

彡

称说：斜三撇

Name: xiésānpiě　　　　ornament

| ノ | ク | 彡 | | 彡 | 彡 | 彡 | 彡 | 彡 | 彡 | 3 |
|---|---|---|---|---|---|---|---|---|---|---|

---

彡　cǎi　multicolour

采 + 彡 = 彩

在"光线"照射下，才可以看到色"彩"。"彡"表示"光彩"，"采"作声旁。
The colour can be seen only in the light. 彡 shows rays of light. 采 is the phonetic component.

| ノ | ヽ | ⺈ | ⺪ | 釆 | 乎 | 乎 | 采 | 彩 | 11 |
|---|---|---|---|---|---|---|---|---|---|

| 彩 | 彩 | 彩 | 彩 | 彩 | 彩 | 彩 | 彩 | 彩 | 彩 |
|---|---|---|---|---|---|---|---|---|---|

---

影　yǐng　shadow

景 + 彡 = 影

"彡"表示光线晃动。光线晃动时才可以看到"影"子。"景"作声旁。
彡 shows rays of light. When there are rays of light, we can see the shadow. 景 is the phonetic component.

| ヽ | 冂 | 冂 | 日 | 旦 | 旦 | 昌 | 景 | 影 | 15 |
|---|---|---|---|---|---|---|---|---|---|

| 影 | 影 | 影 | 影 | 影 | 影 | 影 | 影 | 影 | 影 |
|---|---|---|---|---|---|---|---|---|---|

---

须　xū　beard

彡 + 页 = 须

"彡"表示毛须。"页"表示头。胡须在头上。
彡 shows hair. 页 means head. The beard is on the head.

| 彡 | 彡 | 彡 | 彡 | 须 | 须 | 9 |
|---|---|---|---|---|---|---|

| 须 | 须 | 须 | 须 | 须 | 须 | 须 | 须 | 须 |
|---|---|---|---|---|---|---|---|---|

# 【广部】

广 [廣]　guǎng　　　　　　　　　　　　wide, vast

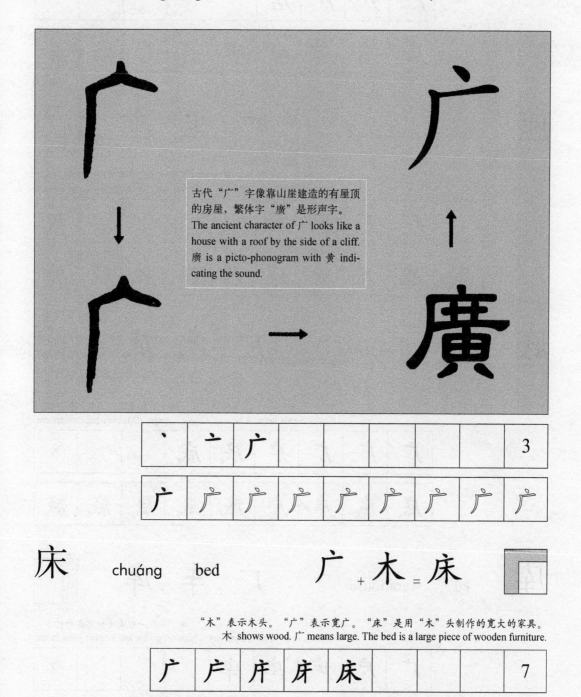

古代"广"字像靠山崖建造的有屋顶的房屋，繁体字"廣"是形声字。
The ancient character of 广 looks like a house with a roof by the side of a cliff. 廣 is a picto-phonogram with 黄 indicating the sound.

| 、 | 宀 | 广 | | | | | | | 3 |
|---|---|---|---|---|---|---|---|---|---|

| 广 | 广 | 广 | 广 | 广 | 广 | 广 | 广 | 广 | 广 |
|---|---|---|---|---|---|---|---|---|---|

床　chuáng　bed　　　　广 + 木 = 床

"木"表示木头。"广"表示宽广。"床"是用"木"头制作的宽大的家具。
木 shows wood. 广 means large. The bed is a large piece of wooden furniture.

| 广 | 广 | 庄 | 庍 | 床 | | | | | 7 |
|---|---|---|---|---|---|---|---|---|---|

| 床 | 床 | 床 | 床 | 床 | 床 | 床 | 床 | 床 |
|---|---|---|---|---|---|---|---|---|

# 店　diàn　shop

广 + 占 = 店

"店"铺是"占"用较大空间的地方。
广 means large. 占 means to occupy. A shop occupies a large space.

| 广 | 疒 | 庐 | 店 | | | | | 8 |
|---|---|---|---|---|---|---|---|---|
| 店 | 店 | 店 | 店 | 店 | 店 | 店 | 店 | 店 |

# 座　zuò　seat, place

广 + 坐 = 座

可以"坐"的，占有一定空间的地方叫"座"位。
广 means a large space. 坐 means to sit. A seat is a space where one can sit.

| 广 | 庂 | 庅 | 座 | | | | | 10 |
|---|---|---|---|---|---|---|---|---|
| 座 | 座 | 座 | 座 | 座 | 座 | 座 | 座 | 座 |

# 底　dǐ　bottom, base

广 + 氏 = 底

某物的"底"部一般较宽大。"氏"作声旁。
广 means large. A base of a thing is large. 氏 is phonetic component.

| 广 | 户 | 庀 | 庍 | 底 | 底 | | | 8 |
|---|---|---|---|---|---|---|---|---|
| 底 | 底 | 底 | 底 | 底 | 底 | 底 | 底 | 底 |

# 库　kù　warehouse

广 + 车 = 库

车"库"一般是个较宽敞的地方。
广 means a large space. 车 means vehicle. A garage has a rather large space.

| 广 | 庁 | 庐 | 庢 | 库 | | | | 7 |
|---|---|---|---|---|---|---|---|---|
| 库 | 库 | 库 | 库 | 库 | 库 | 库 | 库 | 库 |

# 【门部】

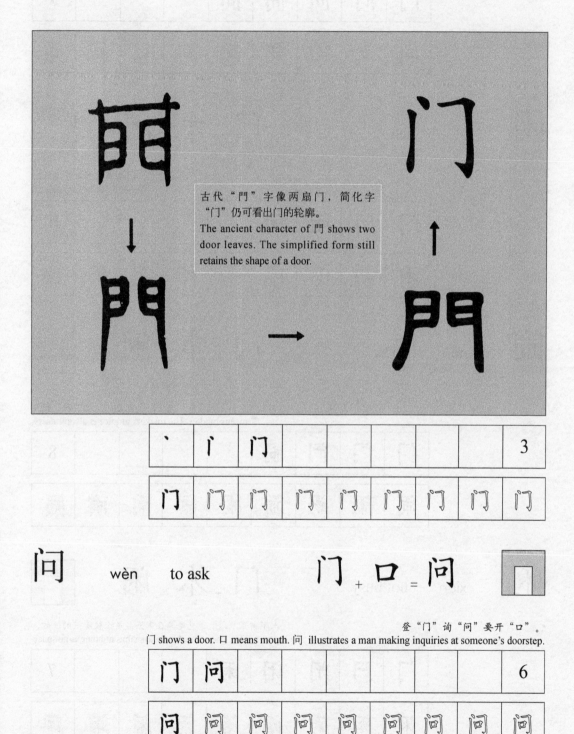

门部的字多和门有关。"门"有时也作声旁。门字旁的位置较固定。
A lot of characters with the radical 门 relate to the door. Sometimes 门 is the phonetic component. Its position is fixed.

门 [門]　　**mén**　　　　　　　　　　　　door

古代"門"字像两扇门，简化字"门"仍可看出门的轮廓。
The ancient character of 門 shows two door leaves. The simplified form still retains the shape of a door.

| 丶 | 冂 | 门 |  |  |  |  |  |  | 3 |

| 门 | 门 | 门 | 门 | 门 | 门 | 门 | 门 | 门 |

问　　**wèn**　　to ask　　　　门 + 口 = 问

登"门"询"问"要开"口"。
门 shows a door. 口 means mouth. 问 illustrates a man making inquiries at someone's doorstep.

| 门 | 问 |  |  |  |  |  |  |  | 6 |

| 问 | 问 | 问 | 问 | 问 | 问 | 问 | 问 | 问 |

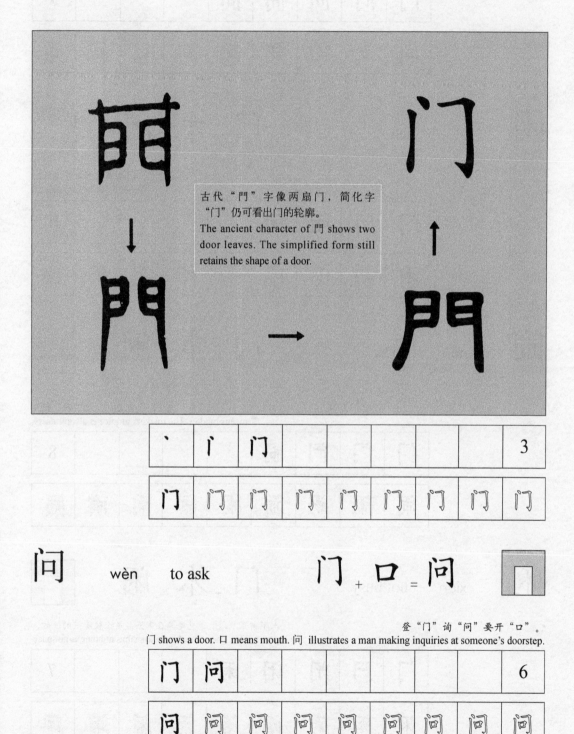

53

# 间　jiān　space

门 + 日 = 间

"日"表示太阳。阳光通过门缝的"间"隙，射入室内。
日 means the sun, which peeps through a crack into a room.

| 门 | 门 | 问 | 间 | 间 | | | 7 |
|---|---|---|---|---|---|---|---|

| 间 | 间 | 间 | 间 | 间 | 间 | 间 | 间 | 间 |
|---|---|---|---|---|---|---|---|---|

# 闭　bì　to close

门 + 才 = 闭

"门"关上叫做"闭"。
The door is closed.

| 门 | 闩 | 闭 | 闭 | | | | 6 |
|---|---|---|---|---|---|---|---|

| 闭 | 闭 | 闭 | 闭 | 闭 | 闭 | 闭 | 闭 | 闭 |
|---|---|---|---|---|---|---|---|---|

# 闹　nào　noisy

门 + 市 = 闹

"市"场"门"口是比较热"闹"的。
市 means market. The market entrance is always noisy.

| 门 | 门 | 闹 | 闹 | | | | 8 |
|---|---|---|---|---|---|---|---|

| 闹 | 闹 | 闹 | 闹 | 闹 | 闹 | 闹 | 闹 | 闹 |
|---|---|---|---|---|---|---|---|---|

# 闲　xián　not busy

门 + 木 = 闲

人不出家"门"，总是呆在家里，是比较清"闲"的。
门 shows a door. The man who always stays at home is not busy.

| 门 | 闩 | 闭 | 闲 | 闲 | | | 7 |
|---|---|---|---|---|---|---|---|

| 闲 | 闲 | 闲 | 闲 | 闲 | 闲 | 闲 | 闲 | 闲 |
|---|---|---|---|---|---|---|---|---|

# 【夕部】

夕部的字有的和夜晚有关。夕字旁的位置较灵活。
Some characters with the radical 夕 relate to night. Its position is flexible.

夕　　　xī　　　　　　　　　　　　　sunset

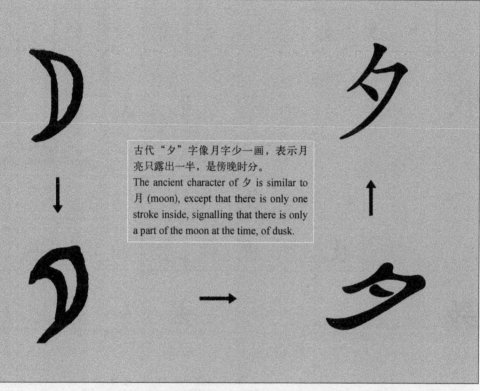

古代"夕"字像月字少一画，表示月亮只露出一半，是傍晚时分。
The ancient character of 夕 is similar to 月 (moon), except that there is only one stroke inside, signalling that there is only a part of the moon at the time, of dusk.

| ノ | ク | 夕 |  |  |  |  |  | 3 |
|---|---|---|---|---|---|---|---|---|

| 夕 | 夕 | 夕 | 夕 | 夕 | 夕 | 夕 | 夕 | 夕 |
|---|---|---|---|---|---|---|---|---|

名　　　míng　　　name　　　　夕 + 口 = 名

"夕"表示傍晚时分。"晚上"招呼人，因看不见，所以要张"口"呼其"名"。
To greet someone at night, you have to open your mouth to call his name, because you can't see him clearly.

| 夕 | 名 |  |  |  |  |  |  | 6 |
|---|---|---|---|---|---|---|---|---|

| 名 | 名 | 名 | 名 | 名 | 名 | 名 | 名 | 名 |
|---|---|---|---|---|---|---|---|---|

# 【攵部】

攵部的字有的和手的动作有关。反文旁一般在字的右侧。
Characters with the radical 攵 refer to the movement of the hand. It is usually placed on the right side.

攵

称说：反文旁
Name: fǎnwénpáng          hand holding a stick

| 丿 | ㇇ | 攵 | 攵 |
|---|---|---|---|

| 攵 | 攵 | 攵 | 攵 | 攵 | 4 |
|---|---|---|---|---|---|

收    shōu    to receive

丩 + 攵 = 收

"收"取东西要用"手"。
Receive something with hand.

| ㇄ | 丩 | 收 | | | 6 |
|---|---|---|---|---|---|

| 收 | 收 | 收 | 收 | 收 | 收 | 收 | 收 | 收 |
|---|---|---|---|---|---|---|---|---|

教    jiāo    to teach

孝 + 攵 = 教

"教"别人掌握某种技能，需要"指手画脚"。"孝"作声旁。
When we teach someone to do something, we usually gesticulate with hands. 孝 is the phonetic component.

| 土 | 耂 | 孝 | 教 | | | 11 |
|---|---|---|---|---|---|---|

| 教 | 教 | 教 | 教 | 教 | 教 | 教 | 教 | 教 |
|---|---|---|---|---|---|---|---|---|

救    jiù    to save

求 + 攵 = 救

"救"人要用"手"。"求"作声旁。
We stretch out a hand to rescue someone. 求 is the phonetic component.

| 一 | 寸 | 寸 | 求 | 求 | 求 | 救 | 11 |
|---|---|---|---|---|---|---|---|

| 救 | 救 | 救 | 救 | 救 | 救 | 救 | 救 | 救 |
|---|---|---|---|---|---|---|---|---|

56

# 【户部】

户部的字多和门户有关。户字旁的位置很固定。
Characters with the radical 户 usually relate to door or household.
Its position is fixed.

户　　　hù　　　single door

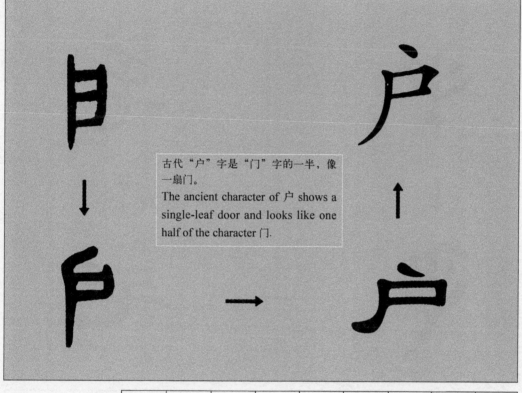

古代"户"字是"门"字的一半，像一扇门。
The ancient character of 户 shows a single-leaf door and looks like one half of the character 门。

| 、 | ⼀ | ⼀ | 户 |  |  |  |  |  | 4 |
|---|---|---|---|---|---|---|---|---|---|

| 户 | 户 | 户 | 户 | 户 | 户 | 户 | 户 | 户 |

房　fáng　house　　

一座"房"子代表一"户"人家。"方"作声旁。
户 means household. A house represents a household. 方 is the phonetic component.

| 户 | 户 | 户 | 房 | 房 |  |  |  | 8 |
|---|---|---|---|---|---|---|---|---|

| 房 | 房 | 房 | 房 | 房 | 房 | 房 | 房 | 房 |

57

# 【毛部】

毛部的字多和毛发或动物的羽毛有关。毛字旁在字的左侧或底部。
Characters with the radical 毛 relate to hair or plume. It is placed on the left side or at the bottom.

毛　　máo　　　　　　　　　　hair

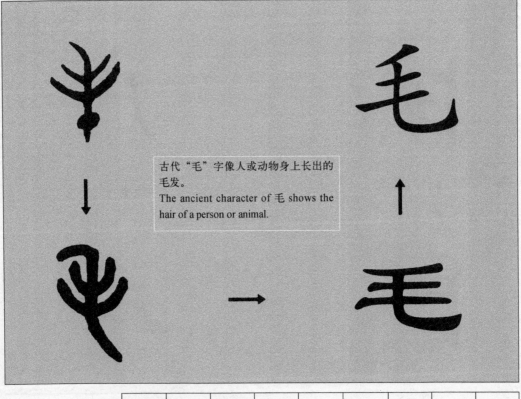

古代"毛"字像人或动物身上长出的毛发。
The ancient character of 毛 shows the hair of a person or animal.

| ㇐ | ㇕ | 三 | 毛 | | | | | 4 |
|---|---|---|---|---|---|---|---|---|
| 毛 | 毛 | 毛 | 毛 | 毛 | 毛 | 毛 | 毛 | 毛 |

笔　　bǐ　　pen

中国的毛"笔"，笔杆是用"竹"子做的，下面是动物的"毛"发。
The handles of Chinese writing brushes are made of bamboo, and the nib is made of hair.

| ノ | ⺮ | ⺮ | 竹 | 竹 | 竹 | 笔 | | 10 |
|---|---|---|---|---|---|---|---|---|
| 笔 | 笔 | 笔 | 笔 | 笔 | 笔 | 笔 | 笔 | 笔 |

58

# 【爪部】

爪部的字多和手和爪有关。爪字旁一般在字的两侧。
Characters with the radical 爪 relate mostly to the hand or claw. It is placed on either side of a character.

爪　　　　　zhǔ　　　　　　　　　　　claw

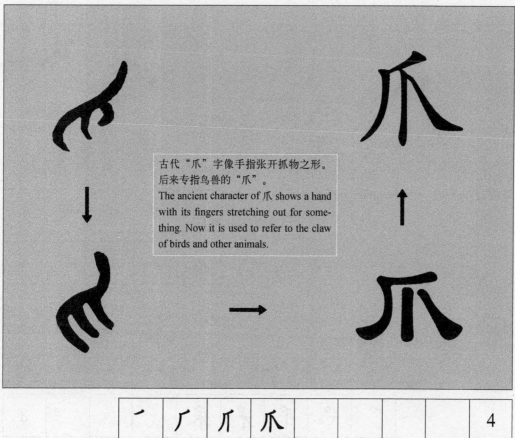

古代"爪"字像手指张开抓物之形。后来专指鸟兽的"爪"。
The ancient character of 爪 shows a hand with its fingers stretching out for something. Now it is used to refer to the claw of birds and other animals.

| ´ | ㄏ | ⺤ | 爪 |  |  |  |  | 4 |

| 爪 | 爪 | 爪 | 爪 | 爪 | 爪 | 爪 | 爪 | 爪 |

爪　　pá　　to crawl

动物"爬"行是要用"爪"的。"巴"作声旁。
爪 shows claw. The animals use their claws to crawl on the ground. 巴 is the phonetic component.

| 爪 | 爬 | 爬 | 爬 | 爬 |  |  |  | 8 |

| 爬 | 爬 | 爬 | 爬 | 爬 | 爬 | 爬 | 爬 | 爬 |

# 【爫部】

"爫" 有由 "爪" 字演变而来。爫部的字多和手和爪的动作有关，其位置在字的上部。

爫 is evolved from 爪. Characters with the radical 爫 mostly refer to the action of the hand or claw. It is placed at the top.

爫

称说：爪字头

Name: zhuǎzìtóu          claw

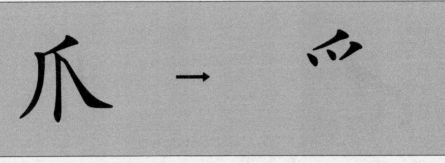

**笔顺及笔画数** Stroke order and number

| ` | ` | ` | ` | 4 |
|---|---|---|---|---|
| ` | ` | ` | ` | ` |

采     cǎi     to pick

"爫" 表示一只手，手指朝下，"木" 表示一棵树。手在树上表示 "采摘" 果实。

爫 shows a hand with the palm downward, and 木 shows a tree. A hand on a tree indicates picking fruit.

| ` | ` | 乎 | 采 | 采 | | | 8 |
|---|---|---|---|---|---|---|---|
| 采 | 采 | 采 | 采 | 采 | 采 | 采 | 采 |

爱     ài     to love

"友" 表示 "友情"。"爱" 一个人是要有 "友情" 的。

爫 shows hand. 友 means friendly sentiments. One who loves another needs hand's caress and sentiments.

| ` | ` | 爫 | 爫 | 严 | 爱 | | 10 |
|---|---|---|---|---|---|---|---|
| 爱 | 爱 | 爱 | 爱 | 爱 | 爱 | 爱 | 爱 |

# 【木部】

木部的字多和树木、木材有关。木字旁在左侧时较多。
Characters with radical 木 relate to tree or wood. It is usually placed on the left side.

木　　　mù　　　　　　　　　　　　tree, wood

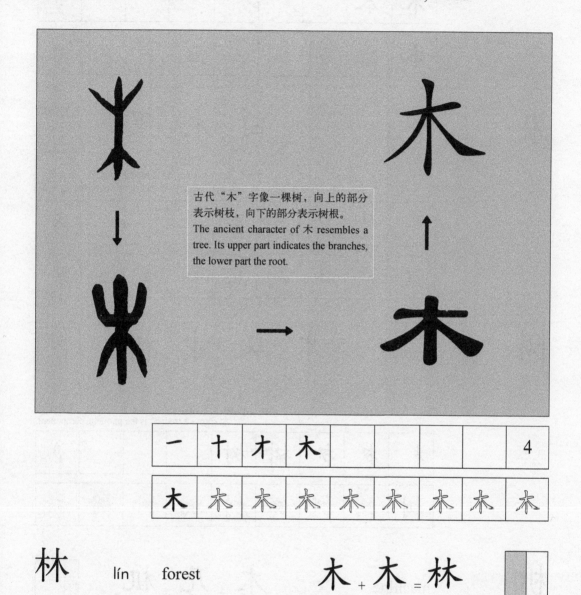

古代"木"字像一棵树，向上的部分表示树枝，向下的部分表示树根。
The ancient character of 木 resembles a tree. Its upper part indicates the branches, the lower part the root.

| 一 | 十 | 才 | 木 | | | | 4 |
|---|---|---|---|---|---|---|---|
| 木 | 木 | 木 | 木 | 木 | 木 | 木 | 木 | 木 |

林　　　lín　　forest　　　　　　木 + 木 = 林

"木"表示一棵树，两棵树在一起表示树木很多。很多树在一起就成树"林"了。
木 shows a tree. Two trees together imply that there are a lot of trees, i.e. a forest.

| 木 | 林 | | | | | | 8 |
|---|---|---|---|---|---|---|---|
| 林 | 林 | 林 | 林 | 林 | 林 | 林 | 林 | 林 |

61

本　běn　root; basic　　木 + 一 = 本

"木"是一棵树，"木"下面的一横指示这儿就"树根"所在的位置。
本 is derived from 木 (tree) to which a horizontal stroke has been added to signify the root.

| 木 | 本 | | | | | | 5 |
|---|---|---|---|---|---|---|---|
| 本 | 本 | 本 | 本 | 本 | 本 | 本 | 本 |

果　guǒ　fruit　　曰 + 木 = 果

"木"表示一棵树。树上结的东西就是"果实"。
木 shows a tree. 果 indicates a tree bearing fruit.

| 丶 | 冂 | 曰 | 曰 | 果 | | | 8 |
|---|---|---|---|---|---|---|---|
| 果 | 果 | 果 | 果 | 果 | 果 | 果 | 果 |

树　shù　tree　　木 + 又 + 寸 = 树

"木"是义旁，"对"是声旁。
木 shows a tree. 对 is the phonetic component.

| 木 | 权 | 权 | 树 | 树 | | | 9 |
|---|---|---|---|---|---|---|---|
| 树 | 树 | 树 | 树 | 树 | 树 | 树 | 树 |

机　jī　machine　　木 + 几 = 机

古代的"机"器是"木"制的。"几"作声旁。
木 shows wood. In the old days, all machines were made of wood. 几 is the phonetic component.

| 木 | 朾 | 机 | | | | | 6 |
|---|---|---|---|---|---|---|---|
| 机 | 机 | 机 | 机 | 机 | 机 | 机 | 机 |

# 【片部】

片部的字大都与木片或木有关。片字旁在字的左侧。
Most characters with the radical 片 relate to wood or wood chips.
It is placed on the left side.

片　　　piàn　　　　　　　　　　　a flat thin piece

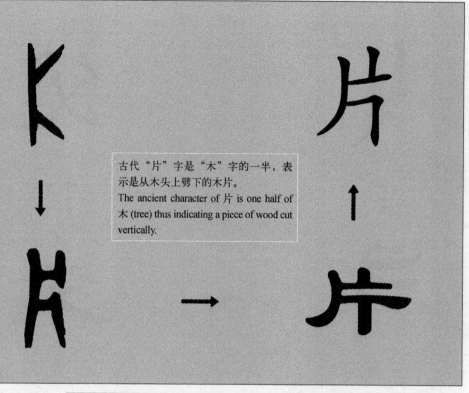

古代"片"字是"木"字的一半，表
示是从木头上劈下的木片。
The ancient character of 片 is one half of
木 (tree) thus indicating a piece of wood cut
vertically.

| ノ | ノ' | ノ' | ア | 片 |  |  |  | 4 |
|---|---|---|---|---|---|---|---|---|
| 片 | 片 | 片 | 片 | 片 | 片 | 片 | 片 | 片 |

牌　　　pái　　plate, card　　　　片 + 卑 = 牌　

"牌"子一般都是"片"状的。"卑"作声旁。
The plate is usually flat and thin. 卑 is the phonetic component.

| 片 | 片' | 片' | 片' | 牌 | 牌 | 牌 | 牌 | 牌 | 12 |
|---|---|---|---|---|---|---|---|---|---|
| 牌 | 牌 | 牌 | 牌 | 牌 | 牌 | 牌 | 牌 | 牌 | 牌 |

# 【父部】

父部的字多表示男性长辈。父字旁一般在字的上部。
Characters with the radical 父 mostly refer to a senior male. It is placed at the top.

父　　fù　　　　　　　　　　　father

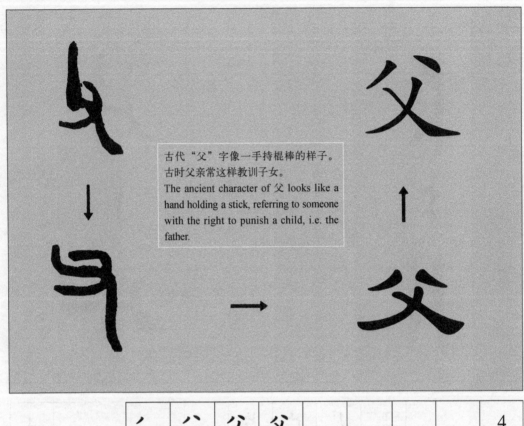

古代"父"字像一手持棍棒的样子。古时父亲常这样教训子女。
The ancient character of 父 looks like a hand holding a stick, referring to someone with the right to punish a child, i.e. the father.

| ノ | ハ | ダ | 父 | | | | | 4 |
|---|---|---|---|---|---|---|---|---|
| 父 | 父 | 父 | 父 | 父 | 父 | 父 | 父 | 父 |

爸　　bà　　dad　　　　　　父 + 巴 = 爸

"父"表示父亲。"巴"作声旁。
父 means father. 巴 is the phonetic component.

| 父 | 父 | 谷 | 谷 | 爸 | | | | 8 |
|---|---|---|---|---|---|---|---|---|
| 爸 | 爸 | 爸 | 爸 | 爸 | 爸 | 爸 | 爸 | 爸 |

64

# 【牛部】

牛部的字多和牛有关。牛字旁多在字的下部。
Characters with the radical 牛 mainly relate to the ox. It is placed at the bottom.

牛　　　niú　　　　　　　　　ox

古代"牛"字像一牛头，上边是翘起的牛角，中间是牛面，两边是牛耳。
The ancient character of 牛 shows the head of an ox, the curves on the top standing for the horns, the vertical stroke the face, and the lower horizontal stroke the two ears.

| 丿 | 广 | 仁 | 牛 | | | | | 4 |
|---|---|---|---|---|---|---|---|---|

| 牛 | 牛 | 牛 | 牛 | 牛 | 牛 | 牛 | 牛 | 牛 |
|---|---|---|---|---|---|---|---|---|

牢　　láo　　prison　　　　宀 + 牛 = 牢

"宀"表示房子。"牢"房像是个关"牛"的房子。
宀 indicates a house. The prison looks like a house where an ox is kept inside.

| 宀 | 牢 | | | | | | | 7 |
|---|---|---|---|---|---|---|---|---|

| 牢 | 牢 | 牢 | 牢 | 牢 | 牢 | 牢 | 牢 | 牢 |
|---|---|---|---|---|---|---|---|---|

# 【牛部】

牛

称说：牛字旁

Name: niúzìpáng          cattle

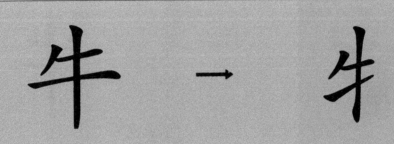

**笔顺及笔画数** Stroke order and number

| ノ | ⺯ | 牛 | 牛 | 4 |
|---|---|---|---|---|
| 牛 | 牛 | 牛 | 牛 | 牛 |

牧  mù  to herd

 牜 + 攵 = 牧

"牛" 羊是要放 "牧" 的。
The cattle and sheep have to be herded.

| 牜 | 牧 |  |  |  |  |  |  | 8 |
|---|---|---|---|---|---|---|---|---|
| 牧 | 牧 | 牧 | 牧 | 牧 | 牧 | 牧 | 牧 | 牧 |

物  wù  thing

牜 + 勿 = 物

"牛" 是一种动 "物"。"勿" 作声旁。
The ox is an animal. 勿 is the phonetic component.

| 牜 | 牜 | 牜 | 物 | 物 |  |  |  | 8 |
|---|---|---|---|---|---|---|---|---|
| 物 | 物 | 物 | 物 | 物 | 物 | 物 | 物 | 物 |

# 【日部】

日部的字多和太阳有关。日字旁在左侧多，也有在上部和下部的。
Characters with the radical 日 relate to the sun. It is usually placed on the left side. In a few cases 日 is also placed at the top or bottom.

日　　　　　　　rì　　　　　　　　　sun

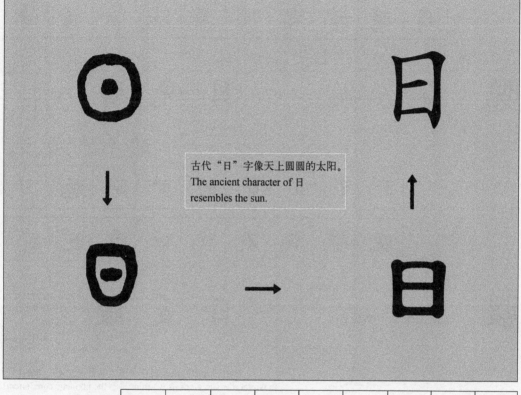

古代"日"字像天上圆圆的太阳。
The ancient character of 日 resembles the sun.

| 丨 | 冂 | 冃 | 日 | | | | | 4 |
|---|---|---|---|---|---|---|---|---|
| 日 | 日 | 日 | 日 | 日 | 日 | 日 | 日 | 日 |

时　　shí　　time　　　　　　　日 + 寸 = 时

根据"太阳"的起落来确定"时"间。
Time is determined by sunrise and sunset.

| 日 | 日一 | 时 | 时 | | | | | 7 |
|---|---|---|---|---|---|---|---|---|
| 时 | 时 | 时 | 时 | 时 | 时 | 时 | 时 | 时 |

# 晴
qíng　　fine day

日 + 青 = 晴

能看到"太阳"日子就是"晴"天。"青"作声旁。
A sunny day is a fine day. 青 is the phonetic component.

| 日 | 日一 | 日二 | 日⺀ | 晴 | 晴 | 晴 | 晴 | 晴 | 12 |
|---|---|---|---|---|---|---|---|---|---|
| 晴 | 晴 | 晴 | 晴 | 晴 | 晴 | 晴 | 晴 | 晴 | |

# 晚
wǎn　　evening

日 + 免 = 晚

"太阳"落山后就到"晚"上了。
Evening begins when the sun sets.

| 日 | 日′ | 日⺈ | 日⺈ | 晄 | 晚 | 晚 | 晚 | | 11 |
|---|---|---|---|---|---|---|---|---|---|
| 晚 | 晚 | 晚 | 晚 | 晚 | 晚 | 晚 | 晚 | 晚 | |

# 暖
nuǎn　　warm

日 + 爰 = 暖

冬天"太阳"给人间带来温"暖"。"爰"作声旁。
In winter, the sun gives us warmth. 爰 is the phonetic component.

| 日 | 日⺊ | 日⺊ | 暖 | 暖 | 暖 | | | | 13 |
|---|---|---|---|---|---|---|---|---|---|
| 暖 | 暖 | 暖 | 暖 | 暖 | 暖 | 暖 | 暖 | 暖 | |

# 春
chūn　　spring

夫 + 日 = 春

"春"天阳光明媚。
In spring, the sun is bright.

| 一 | 二 | 三 | 丰 | 夫 | 春 | | | | 9 |
|---|---|---|---|---|---|---|---|---|---|
| 春 | 春 | 春 | 春 | 春 | 春 | 春 | 春 | 春 | |

# 【月部】

月作偏旁代表两个字，一是月亮的"月"，一是"肉"字。月部的字，"月"在右侧的字多和月亮有关，"月"在左侧的字多和人体有关。

月 represents two characters. One is 月 (moon) and the other is 肉 (meat). Characters with the radical 月 on the right side relate to the moon, and those with 月 on the left side relate to the body.

月　　　yuè　　　　　　　　　moon, month

古代"月"字像夜空中弯弯的月亮。
The ancient character of 月 looks like a crescent at night.

| 丿 | 几 | 月 | 月 | | | | | 4 |
|---|---|---|---|---|---|---|---|---|

| 月 | 月 | 月 | 月 | 月 | 月 | 月 | 月 | 月 |
|---|---|---|---|---|---|---|---|---|

明　　　míng　　bright　　　日 + 月 = 明

"太阳"和"月亮"都给人带来光"明"。
日 means the sun. The sun and moon together bring brightness to people.

| 日 | 明 | | | | | | | 8 |
|---|---|---|---|---|---|---|---|---|

| 明 | 明 | 明 | 明 | 明 | 明 | 明 | 明 | 明 |
|---|---|---|---|---|---|---|---|---|

# 朋  péng  friend

月 + 月 = 朋

"月月"都来就成了"朋"友。
月 means month. A person who visits every month becomes a friend.

| 月 | 朋 | | | | | | | 8 |
|---|---|---|---|---|---|---|---|---|
| 朋 | 朋 | 朋 | 朋 | 朋 | 朋 | 朋 | 朋 | 朋 |

# 肚  dù  belly

月 + 土 = 肚

"肚"子是人体的一部分。"土"作声旁。
月 shows body. The belly is part of the body. 土 is the phonetic component.

| 月 | 肚 | | | | | | | 7 |
|---|---|---|---|---|---|---|---|---|
| 肚 | 肚 | 肚 | 肚 | 肚 | 肚 | 肚 | 肚 | 肚 |

# 服  fú  clothes

月 + 艮 = 服

衣"服"是穿在人"身体"上的。
月 shows body. The clothes are put on the body.

| 月 | 月' | 朋 | 服 | | | | | 8 |
|---|---|---|---|---|---|---|---|---|
| 服 | 服 | 服 | 服 | 服 | 服 | 服 | 服 | 服 |

# 脚  jiǎo  foot

月 + 去 + 卩 = 脚

"脚"是人体的一部分。"却"作声旁。
月 shows body. The foot is part of the body. 却 is the phonetic component.

| 月 | 胜 | 胠 | 脐 | 脚 | | | | 11 |
|---|---|---|---|---|---|---|---|---|
| 脚 | 脚 | 脚 | 脚 | 脚 | 脚 | 脚 | 脚 | 脚 |

# 【手部】

手部的字和手有关。手字旁一般在字的下部。
Characters with the radical 手 relate to hand. It is usually placed at the bottom.

手　　　　shǒu　　　　　　　　　　hand

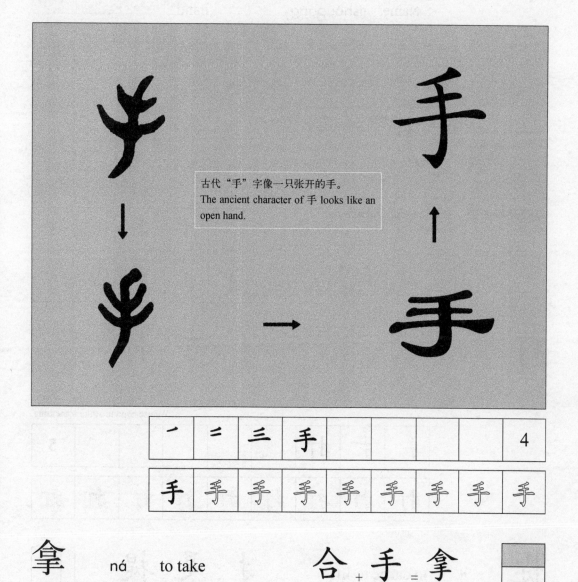

古代"手"字像一只张开的手。
The ancient character of 手 looks like an open hand.

| 一 | 二 | 三 | 手 | | | | | 4 |
|---|---|---|---|---|---|---|---|---|
| 手 | 手 | 手 | 手 | 手 | 手 | 手 | 手 | 手 |

拿　　　ná　　to take　　　　合 + 手 = 拿

把"手"掌"合"起来才可以"拿"东西。
合 means to close. We close our hands to take something.

| 人 | 合 | 合 | 拿 | | | | | 10 |
|---|---|---|---|---|---|---|---|---|
| 拿 | 拿 | 拿 | 拿 | 拿 | 拿 | 拿 | 拿 | 拿 |

71

# 【扌部】

"扌"是由"手"字演变而来。扌部的字和手的动作有关。提手旁在字的左侧。
扌 is evolved from 手. Characters with the radical 扌 refer to hand's action. It is placed on the left side.

扌　　称说：提手旁
　　　Name: tíshǒupáng　　　　　hand

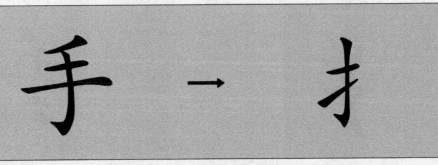

**笔顺及笔画数** Stroke order and number

| 一 | 丁 | 扌 | | 3 |
|---|---|---|---|---|

| 扌 | 扌 | 扌 | 扌 | 扌 |
|---|---|---|---|---|

打　dǎ　to strike, to hit　　扌 + 丁 = 打

用"手"来击"打"东西。
We use hand to strike something.

| 扌 | 才 | 打 | | | | | 5 |
|---|---|---|---|---|---|---|---|

| 打 | 打 | 打 | 打 | 打 | 打 | 打 | 打 | 打 |
|---|---|---|---|---|---|---|---|---|

提　tí　to carry, to lift　　扌 + 是 = 提

用"手"把东西"提"起来。
We use hand to carry something.

| 扌 | 扣 | 担 | 捍 | 捍 | 提 | | 12 |
|---|---|---|---|---|---|---|---|

| 提 | 提 | 提 | 提 | 提 | 提 | 提 | 提 | 提 |
|---|---|---|---|---|---|---|---|---|

# 【火部】

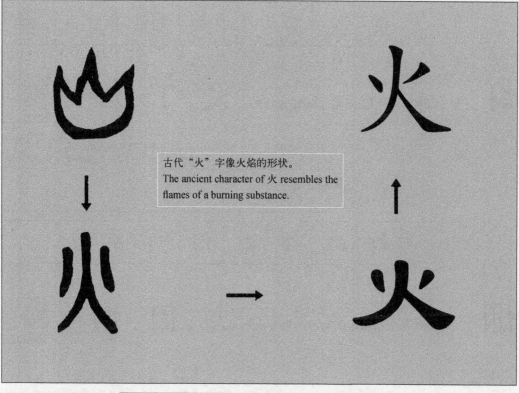

火部的字多和火有关。火字旁一般在字的左侧或上下。
Characters with the radical 火 relate to fire. It is usually placed on the left side, or at the bottom or top.

火　　　huǒ　　　　　　　　　　　fire

古代"火"字像火焰的形状。
The ancient character of 火 resembles the flames of a burning substance.

| 、 | 丷 | 少 | 火 | | | | | 4 |
|---|---|---|---|---|---|---|---|---|
| 火 | 火 | 火 | 火 | 火 | 火 | 火 | 火 | 火 |

烧　　　shāo　　　to burn　　　火 + 尧 = 烧　　

"火"可以燃烧。"尧"作声旁。
The fire can burn. 尧 is the phonetic component.

| 火 | 灯 | 灼 | 炷 | 烤 | 烧 | | | | 10 |
|---|---|---|---|---|---|---|---|---|---|
| 烧 | 烧 | 烧 | 烧 | 烧 | 烧 | 烧 | 烧 | 烧 |

**炎** yán scorching 火 + 火 = 炎

两个"火"字,一个在上,一个在下,表示火势很大。
火 means fire; and one fire on top of the other depicts scorching heat.

| 火 | 炎 | | | | | | | 8 |
|---|---|---|---|---|---|---|---|---|
| 炎 | 炎 | 炎 | 炎 | 炎 | 炎 | 炎 | 炎 | 炎 |

**灯** dēng lantern, lamp 火 + 丁 = 灯

古时的灯笼是用"火"来照明的。
In ancient times, the lantern illuminates with fire. 丁 is the phonetic component.

| 火 | 火 | 灯 | | | | | | 6 |
|---|---|---|---|---|---|---|---|---|
| 灯 | 灯 | 灯 | 灯 | 灯 | 灯 | 灯 | 灯 | 灯 |

**烟** yān smoke 火 + 因 = 烟

"烟"是由"火"产生的。"因"作声旁。
Smoke comes from fire. 因 is the phonetic component.

| 火 | 灼 | 烔 | 烟 | 烟 | | | | 10 |
|---|---|---|---|---|---|---|---|---|
| 烟 | 烟 | 烟 | 烟 | 烟 | 烟 | 烟 | 烟 | 烟 |

**灭** miè (of a fire) go out 一 + 火 = 灭

"一"表示在火焰上方压个东西,这样"火"就熄灭了。
一 shows that we use something to cover the fire in order to extinguish it.

| 一 | 灭 | | | | | | | 5 |
|---|---|---|---|---|---|---|---|---|
| 灭 | 灭 | 灭 | 灭 | 灭 | 灭 | 灭 | 灭 | 灭 |

# 【灬部】

"灬"是"火"字的变体。灬字旁在字的下部。
灬 is a variant of 火. Characters with the radical 灬 relate to fire. It is placed at the bottom.

灬　　　称说：四点底
　　　　Name: sìdiǎndǐ　　　　fire

**笔顺及笔画数**　Stroke order and number

| ` | `` | ``` | ```` | 4 |
|---|---|---|---|---|

| 灬 | 灬 | 灬 | 灬 | 灬 |
|---|---|---|---|---|

热　rè　hot; heat　

"火"产生热量。"执"作声旁。
Fire produces heat. 执 is the phonetic component.

| 扌 | 扮 | 执 | 执 | 热 | | | | | 10 |
|---|---|---|---|---|---|---|---|---|---|

| 热 | 热 | 热 | 热 | 热 | 热 | 热 | 热 | 热 |
|---|---|---|---|---|---|---|---|---|

点　diǎn　to light; point　

"点"有点燃的意思，火可以点燃物品。"占"作声旁。
点 means to light a fire. The fire can light something. 占 is the phonetic component.

| ` | 卜 | 占 | 点 | | | | | | 9 |
|---|---|---|---|---|---|---|---|---|---|

| 点 | 点 | 点 | 点 | 点 | 点 | 点 | 点 | 点 |
|---|---|---|---|---|---|---|---|---|

# 【水部】

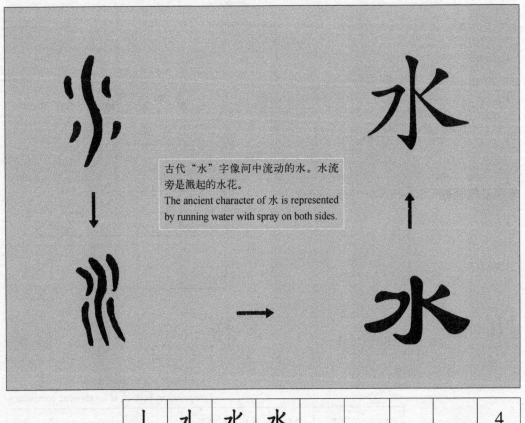

水部的字多和水有关。水字旁在字的下部或上部。
Characters with the radical 水 relate to water. It is placed at the top or bottom.

水　　　shuǐ　　　　　　　　　water

古代"水"字像河中流动的水。水流旁是溅起的水花。
The ancient character of 水 is represented by running water with spray on both sides.

| ↓ | 刀 | 水 | 水 | | | | | 4 |
|---|---|---|---|---|---|---|---|---|
| 水 | 水 | 水 | 水 | 水 | 水 | 水 | 水 | 水 |

尿　　niào　urine　　　　　　尸 + 水 = 尿

"尸"表示身体。"尿"是从体内排泄出的"水分"。
尸 means body. Urine is the water that is excreted through organs of body.

| 尸 | 尿 | | | | | | | 7 |
|---|---|---|---|---|---|---|---|---|
| 尿 | 尿 | 尿 | 尿 | 尿 | 尿 | 尿 | 尿 | 尿 |

# 【氵部】

氵

称说：三点水

Name: sāndiǎnshuǐ         water

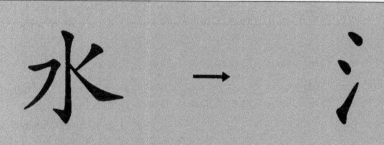

笔顺及笔画数   Stroke order and number

| 、 | 冫 | 氵 | | 3 |
|---|---|---|---|---|
| 氵 | 氵 | 氵 | 氵 | 氵 |

---

河    hé    river

氵 + 可 = 河

"水"流成"河"。"可"作声旁。

氵 shows water. The flowing water becomes a river. 可 is the phonetic component.

| 氵 | 氵 | 沪 | 河 | | | | | 8 |
|---|---|---|---|---|---|---|---|---|
| 河 | 河 | 河 | 河 | 河 | 河 | 河 | 河 | 河 |

---

江    jiāng    river

氵 + 工 = 江

大河称其为"江"。

A great river is 江.

| 氵 | 江 | | | | | | | 6 |
|---|---|---|---|---|---|---|---|---|
| 江 | 江 | 江 | 江 | 江 | 江 | 江 | 江 | 江 |

77

海 hǎi sea

氵 + 每 = 海

"海"水的主要成分是"水"。
氵 shows water. The principal element of the sea is water.

| 氵 | 氵 | 汇 | 汇 | 海 | 海 | 海 | 海 | 10 |
|---|---|---|---|---|---|---|---|---|
| 海 | 海 | 海 | 海 | 海 | 海 | 海 | 海 | 海 |

油 yóu oil

氵 + 由 = 油

"油"是像"水"一样的液体。"由"作声旁。
氵 shows liquid. Oil is a liquid. 由 is the phonetic component.

| 氵 | 氵 | 汀 | 汩 | 油 | 油 | | | 8 |
|---|---|---|---|---|---|---|---|---|
| 油 | 油 | 油 | 油 | 油 | 油 | 油 | 油 | 油 |

活 huó to live

氵 + 舌 = 活

没有"水"就没有"生命"。
氵 shows water. Where there is no water, there is no life.

| 氵 | 氵 | 汓 | 汗 | 活 | | | | 9 |
|---|---|---|---|---|---|---|---|---|
| 活 | 活 | 活 | 活 | 活 | 活 | 活 | 活 | 活 |

洗 xǐ to wash

氵 + 先 = 洗

用"水"来"洗"东西。
氵 shows water. We use water to wash things.

| 氵 | 氵 | 氵 | 汫 | 洴 | 洗 | | | 9 |
|---|---|---|---|---|---|---|---|---|
| 洗 | 洗 | 洗 | 洗 | 洗 | 洗 | 洗 | 洗 | 洗 |

78

# 【贝部】

贝部的字多和钱财、交易有关。贝字旁的位置较灵活。
Characters with the radical 贝 refer to money, wealth and trade. Its position is flexible.

## 贝［貝］ bèi    seashell

古代"贝"字像海中的贝壳。贝壳古代曾用作货币。
The ancient character of 贝 shows the ventral view of a shell. In the early stages of civilization, shells were used as money.

| 丨 | 冂 | 刂 | 贝 | | | | | 4 |
|---|---|---|---|---|---|---|---|---|
| 贝 | 贝 | 贝 | 贝 | 贝 | 贝 | 贝 | 贝 | 贝 |

## 财 cái wealth

贝 + 才 = 财

"财"产以金钱货币来计算。"才"作声旁。
Wealth is calculated with money. 才 is the phonetic component.

| 贝 | 贝 | 财 | 财 | | | | | 7 |
|---|---|---|---|---|---|---|---|---|
| 财 | 财 | 财 | 财 | 财 | 财 | 财 | 财 | 财 |

79

# 购 gòu to buy

贝 + 勾 = 购

"购"买商品要用货币。"勾"作声旁。
Buying something with money. 勾 is the phonetic component.

| 贝 | 贝 | 贴 | 购 | 购 | | | 8 |
|---|---|---|---|---|---|---|---|

| 购 | 购 | 购 | 购 | 购 | 购 | 购 | 购 | 购 |
|---|---|---|---|---|---|---|---|---|

# 贵 guì expensive

中 + 一 + 贝 = 贵

古代"贝壳"是一种"贵"重的饰物。
贝 means seashell. In ancient times, shell was an expensive ornament.

| 口 | 中 | 虫 | 贵 | | | | | 9 |
|---|---|---|---|---|---|---|---|---|

| 贵 | 贵 | 贵 | 贵 | 贵 | 贵 | 贵 | 贵 | 贵 |
|---|---|---|---|---|---|---|---|---|

# 费 fèi fee

弗 + 贝 = 费

"费"用就是指所花的"钱"的多少。"弗"作声旁。
贝 shows money. The fee means payment for a service. 弗 is the phonetic component.

| 弓 | 弗 | 弗 | 费 | | | | | 9 |
|---|---|---|---|---|---|---|---|---|

| 费 | 费 | 费 | 费 | 费 | 费 | 费 | 费 | 费 |
|---|---|---|---|---|---|---|---|---|

# 货 huò goods

化 + 贝 = 货

用"金钱"购买的东西称为"货"物。
贝 shows money. Goods are things bought with money.

| 亻 | 仁 | 化 | 货 | | | | | 8 |
|---|---|---|---|---|---|---|---|---|

| 货 | 货 | 货 | 货 | 货 | 货 | 货 | 货 | 货 |
|---|---|---|---|---|---|---|---|---|

# 【车部】

车部的字多和车有关。车字旁的位置一般在字的左侧。
Characters with the radical 车 refer to vehicles. It is usually placed on the left side.

## 车 [車] chē          vehicle

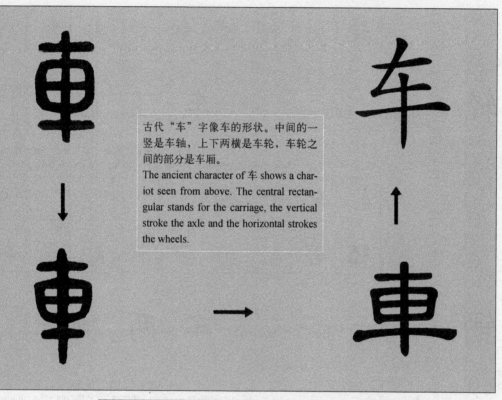

古代"车"字像车的形状。中间的一竖是车轴，上下两横是车轮，车轮之间的部分是车厢。
The ancient character of 车 shows a chariot seen from above. The central rectangular stands for the carriage, the vertical stroke the axle and the horizontal strokes the wheels.

| 一 | 七 | 产 | 车 | | | | | 4 |
|---|---|---|---|---|---|---|---|---|
| 车 | 车 | 车 | 车 | 车 | 车 | 车 | 车 | 车 |

## 轮 lún wheel      车 + 仑 = 轮

"轮"子是"车"的一部分。"仑"作声旁。
The wheel is part of a vehicle. 仑 is the phonetic component.

| 车 | 轮 | 轮 | 轮 | | | | | 8 |
|---|---|---|---|---|---|---|---|---|
| 轮 | 轮 | 轮 | 轮 | 轮 | 轮 | 轮 | 轮 | 轮 |

# 转 zhuàn    to turn

车 + 专 = 转

"车子"是可以"转"动的。"专"作声旁。
The vehicle can turn. 专 is the phonetic component.

| 车 | 车 | 车 | 转 | 转 | | | 8 |
|---|---|---|---|---|---|---|---|

| 转 | 转 | 转 | 转 | 转 | 转 | 转 | 转 | 转 |
|---|---|---|---|---|---|---|---|---|

# 轻 qīng    light

车 + 圣 = 轻

驾"车"行驶比走路要"轻"快。"圣"作声旁。
Travelling by vehicle is lighter than walking. 圣 is the phonetic component.

| 车 | 轵 | 轵 | 轻 | | | | 9 |
|---|---|---|---|---|---|---|---|

| 轻 | 轻 | 轻 | 轻 | 轻 | 轻 | 轻 | 轻 | 轻 |
|---|---|---|---|---|---|---|---|---|

# 辆 liàng    (a measure word)

车 + 两 = 辆

"辆"是表示"车"的量词。"两"作声旁。
辆 is a measure word for vehicles. 两 is the phonetic component.

| 车 | 车 | 车 | 轫 | 辆 | 辆 | | 11 |
|---|---|---|---|---|---|---|---|

| 辆 | 辆 | 辆 | 辆 | 辆 | 辆 | 辆 | 辆 | 辆 |
|---|---|---|---|---|---|---|---|---|

# 军 jūn    army

冖 + 车 = 军

"军"队都是有战"车"的。
The army possesses the war chariot.

| 丶 | 冖 | 军 | | | | | 6 |
|---|---|---|---|---|---|---|---|

| 军 | 军 | 军 | 军 | 军 | 军 | 军 | 军 | 军 |
|---|---|---|---|---|---|---|---|---|

82

# 【戈部】

戈部的字有的和武器、战争有关。戈字旁在字的两侧。
Characters with the radical 戈 refer to weapons and war. It is placed on either side.

戈　　　　gē　　　　　　　　　　　dagger-axe

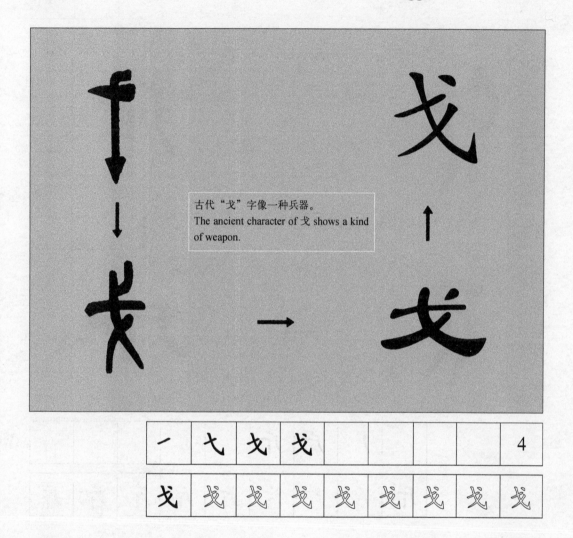

古代"戈"字像一种兵器。
The ancient character of 戈 shows a kind of weapon.

| 一 | 七 | 戋 | 戈 | | | | | 4 |
|---|---|---|---|---|---|---|---|---|

| 戈 | 戈 | 戈 | 戈 | 戈 | 戈 | 戈 | 戈 | 戈 |
|---|---|---|---|---|---|---|---|---|

战　　zhàn　　fight, war　　　　占 + 戈 = 战　　

作"战"要用"兵器"。"占"作声旁。
People use weapon to wage a war. 占 is the phonetic component.

| 丨 | 卜 | 占 | 战 | | | | | 9 |
|---|---|---|---|---|---|---|---|---|

| 战 | 战 | 战 | 战 | 战 | 战 | 战 | 战 | 战 |
|---|---|---|---|---|---|---|---|---|

# 【斤部】

斤部的字多和斧子或砍折有关。斤字旁多在字的右侧。
Characters with the radical 斤 relate to the axe or chopping. It is usually placed on the right side.

斤　　　jīn　　　　　　　　　axe

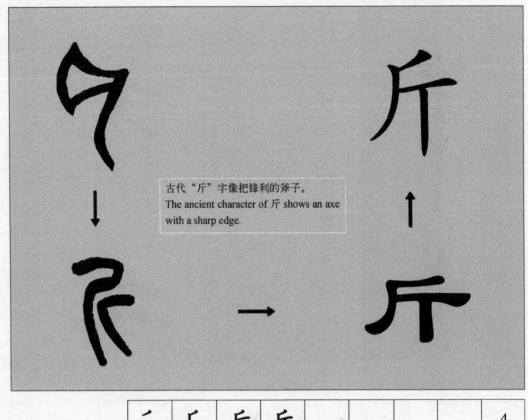

古代"斤"字像把锋利的斧子。
The ancient character of 斤 shows an axe with a sharp edge.

| ´ | 厂 | 斤 | 斤 | | | | | 4 |
|---|---|---|---|---|---|---|---|---|

| 斤 | 斤 | 斤 | 斤 | 斤 | 斤 | 斤 | 斤 | 斤 |
|---|---|---|---|---|---|---|---|---|

断　　　duàn　　to break　　　　迷 + 斤 = 断

"斤"表示斧子。用斧子才可以把东西砍"断"。
斤 shows an axe. The axe can be used to break off something.

| 丶 | 丷 | 丷 | 半 | 半 | 米 | 迷 | 断 | 11 |
|---|---|---|---|---|---|---|---|---|

| 断 | 断 | 断 | 断 | 断 | 断 | 断 | 断 | 断 |
|---|---|---|---|---|---|---|---|---|

# 【气部】

气部的字多和气体有关。气字旁的位置较固定。
Characters with the radical 气 refer to gas. Its position is fixed.

气 [氣] qì                                         air

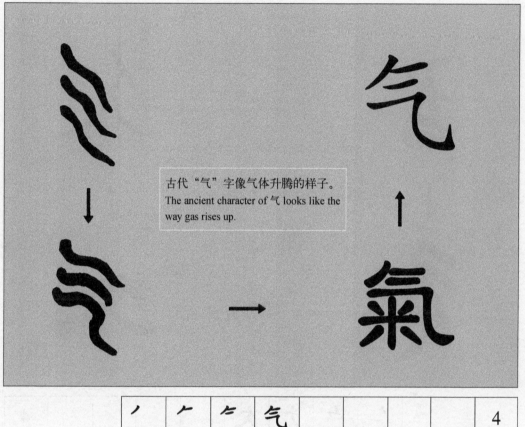

古代"气"字像气体升腾的样子。
The ancient character of 气 looks like the way gas rises up.

| ノ | ￢ | ⌐ | 气 | | | | | 4 |
|---|---|---|---|---|---|---|---|---|
| 气 | 气 | 气 | 气 | 气 | 气 | 气 | 气 | 气 |

氧 yǎng oxygen          气 + 羊 = 氧

"氧"是一种气体。"羊"作声旁。
Oxygen is a gas. 羊 is the phonetic component.

| 气 | 气 | 氜 | 氜 | 氜 | 氢 | 氧 | | 10 |
|---|---|---|---|---|---|---|---|---|
| 氧 | 氧 | 氧 | 氧 | 氧 | 氧 | 氧 | 氧 | 氧 |

# 【欠部】

欠部的字多和用嘴出气有关。欠字旁的位置一般在字的右侧。
Characters with the radical 欠 refer to exhalation. It is usually placed on the right side.

欠　　　qiàn　　　　　　　　　　　　　　　　　to yawn, to owe

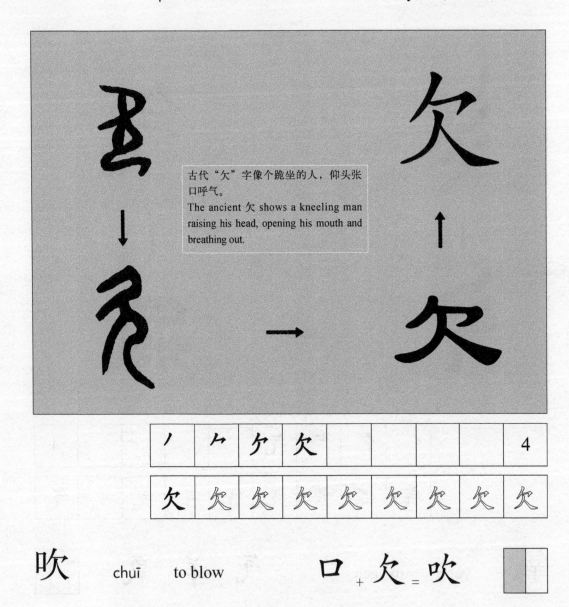

古代"欠"字像个跪坐的人，仰头张口呼气。
The ancient 欠 shows a kneeling man raising his head, opening his mouth and breathing out.

| ノ | 𠂉 | 𠂆 | 欠 | | | | | 4 |
|---|---|---|---|---|---|---|---|---|

| 欠 | 欠 | 欠 | 欠 | 欠 | 欠 | 欠 | 欠 | 欠 |
|---|---|---|---|---|---|---|---|---|

吹　　　chuī　　　to blow　　　　　　口 + 欠 = 吹

"口"表示嘴。"吹"的动作是用嘴出气。
口 means mouth. Blowing looks like an exhalation with the mouth.

| 口 | 吹 | | | | | | | 7 |
|---|---|---|---|---|---|---|---|---|

| 吹 | 吹 | 吹 | 吹 | 吹 | 吹 | 吹 | 吹 | 吹 |
|---|---|---|---|---|---|---|---|---|

# 【犬部】

犬部的字和狗有关。犬字旁在字的下面。
Characters with the radical 犬 are relevant to dogs. It is usually placed at the bottom.

犬　　　quǎn　　　　　　　　　　　dog

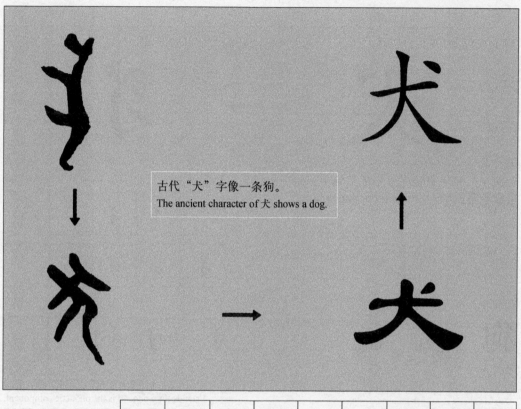

古代"犬"字像一条狗。
The ancient character of 犬 shows a dog.

| 一 | ナ | 大 | 犬 | | | | | 4 |
|---|---|---|---|---|---|---|---|---|

| 犬 | 犬 | 犬 | 犬 | 犬 | 犬 | 犬 | 犬 | 犬 |
|---|---|---|---|---|---|---|---|---|

哭　　kū　　to cry　　口 + 口 + 犬 = 哭

人"哭"时，其声音像"狗"叫。
When a person cries, he sounds the same as dog's cry.

| 口 | 吅 | 哭 | | | | | | 10 |
|---|---|---|---|---|---|---|---|---|

| 哭 | 哭 | 哭 | 哭 | 哭 | 哭 | 哭 | 哭 | 哭 |
|---|---|---|---|---|---|---|---|---|

# 【犭部】

"犭" 是由 "犬" 字演变而来的。犭部的字多和兽类有关。反犬旁在字的左侧。

犭 is evolved from 犬 (dog). Characters with the radical 犭 refer to animals. It is placed on the left side.

犭　　称说：反犬旁
　　　Name: fǎnquǎnpáng　　animal

**笔顺及笔画数**　Stroke order and number

| ノ | 犭 | 犭 | | 3 |
|---|---|---|---|---|

| 犭 | 犭 | 犭 | 犭 | 犭 |
|---|---|---|---|---|

狗　　gǒu　dog　　　　

"犭" 表示 "狗"。"句" 作声旁。
犭 stands for a dog. 句 is the phonetic component.

| 犭 | 犭 | 犳 | 狗 | | | | 8 |
|---|---|---|---|---|---|---|---|

| 狗 | 狗 | 狗 | 狗 | 狗 | 狗 | 狗 | 狗 | 狗 |
|---|---|---|---|---|---|---|---|---|

猫　　māo　cat　　　　犭 + 苗 = 猫

"猫" 是种动物。"苗" 作声旁。
A cat is an animal. 苗 is the phonetic component.

| 犭 | 犭 | 犭 | 猫 | 猫 | 猫 | 猫 | 11 |
|---|---|---|---|---|---|---|---|

| 猫 | 猫 | 猫 | 猫 | 猫 | 猫 | 猫 | 猫 | 猫 |
|---|---|---|---|---|---|---|---|---|

# 【文部】

文　wén　script, writing

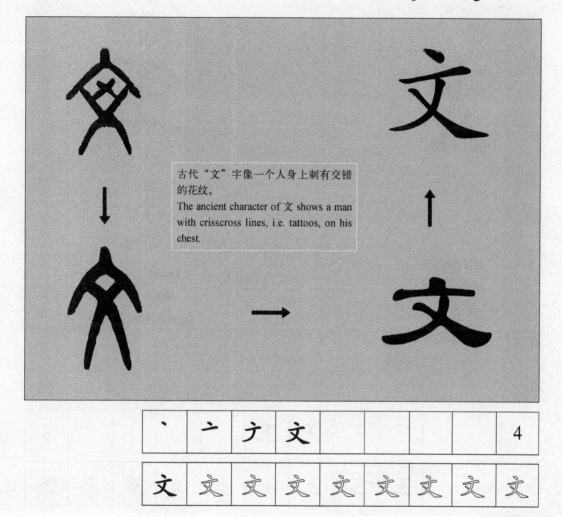

古代"文"字像一个人身上刺有交错的花纹。

The ancient character of 文 shows a man with crisscross lines, i.e. tattoos, on his chest.

| 、 | 一 | 亠 | 文 | | | | | 4 |
|---|---|---|---|---|---|---|---|---|
| 文 | 文 | 文 | 文 | 文 | 文 | 文 | 文 | 文 |

齐　qí　in good order

文 + 八 = 齐

"文"字一般都是整"齐"地排列着。
Writing is normally done in good order.

| 文 | 齐 | 齐 | | | | | | 6 |
|---|---|---|---|---|---|---|---|---|
| 齐 | 齐 | 齐 | 齐 | 齐 | 齐 | 齐 | 齐 | 齐 |

89

# 【王部】

王部的字多和王或玉有关。王字旁多在字的左侧。
Characters with the radical 王 mostly relate to king or jade. It is placed on the left side.

王　　　wáng　　　　　　　　　　　king, jade

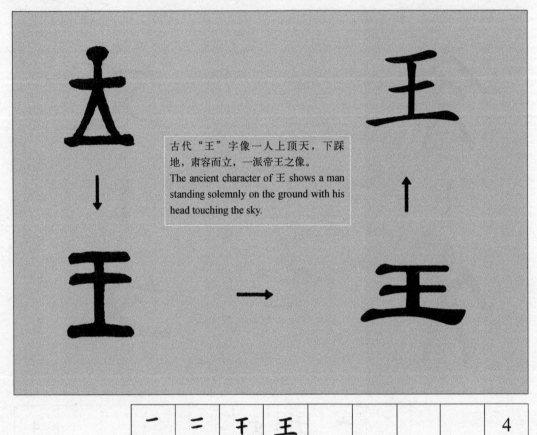

古代"王"字像一人上顶天，下踩地，肃容而立，一派帝王之像。
The ancient character of 王 shows a man standing solemnly on the ground with his head touching the sky.

| 一 | 二 | 干 | 王 |  |  |  |  | 4 |
|---|---|---|---|---|---|---|---|---|
| 王 | 王 | 王 | 王 | 王 | 王 | 王 | 王 | 王 |

主　　　zhǔ　　master, host　　　　　` + 王 = 主

国"王"乃一国之"主"。
王 means king. A king is the master of a country.

| ` | 主 |  |  |  |  |  |  | 5 |
|---|---|---|---|---|---|---|---|---|
| 主 | 主 | 主 | 主 | 主 | 主 | 主 | 主 | 主 |

90

# 【心部】

心　　xīn　　　　　　　　　　heart

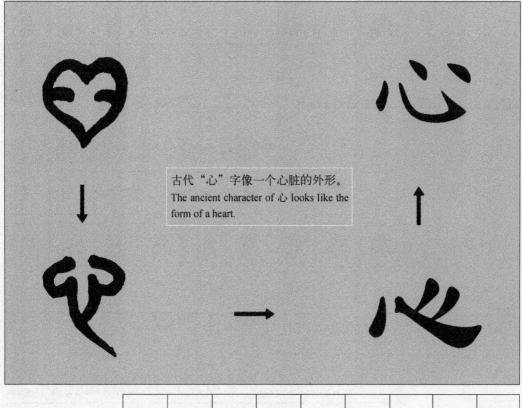

古代"心"字像一个心脏的外形。
The ancient character of 心 looks like the form of a heart.

| ﹑ | 心 | 心 | 心 | | | | | 4 |
|---|---|---|---|---|---|---|---|---|
| 心 | 心 | 心 | 心 | 心 | 心 | 心 | 心 | 心 |

想　　xiǎng　to think　　　相 + 心 = 想　

"想"是心理活动。"相"作声旁。
Thinking is a mental activity. 相 is the phonetic component.

| 木 | 朩 | 村 | 相 | 相 | 相 | 想 | 13 |
|---|---|---|---|---|---|---|---|
| 想 | 想 | 想 | 想 | 想 | 想 | 想 | 想 |

91

# 念 niàn  to miss

今 + 心 = 念

思"念"是心理活动。
To miss someone is a mental activity.

| 人 | 人 | 今 | 念 | | | | 8 |
|---|---|---|---|---|---|---|---|
| 念 | 念 | 念 | 念 | 念 | 念 | 念 | 念 | 念 |

# 忘 wàng  to forget

亡 + 心 = 忘

"亡"是死亡的意思。记在"心"里的事情消失了，就是"忘"了。
亡 means to die. To forget something means that the thing is dead in the heart.

| 丶 | 亠 | 亡 | 忘 | | | | 7 |
|---|---|---|---|---|---|---|---|
| 忘 | 忘 | 忘 | 忘 | 忘 | 忘 | 忘 | 忘 | 忘 |

# 您 nín  you (respectful)

你 + 心 = 您

"你"是表示第二人称单数的代词。下面加"心"表示敬称。
你 is a singular pronoun in the 2nd person, and 心 (heart) is added to show respect.

| 亻 | 亻 | 伂 | 你 | 您 | | | 11 |
|---|---|---|---|---|---|---|---|
| 您 | 您 | 您 | 您 | 您 | 您 | 您 | 您 | 您 |

# 思 sī  to think deeply

田 + 心 = 思

"思"考问题是心理活动。
To think deeply is a mental activity.

| 丨 | 冂 | 日 | 田 | 田 | 思 | | 9 |
|---|---|---|---|---|---|---|---|
| 思 | 思 | 思 | 思 | 思 | 思 | 思 | 思 | 思 |

# 【忄部】

"忄"是由"心"字演变而来。忄部的字和心理活动有关。忄的位置在字的左侧。

忄 is evolved from 心. Characters with the radical 忄 also refer to mental activities. It is placed on the left side.

忄　　称说：竖心旁

Name: shùxīnpáng　　　　heart

心 → 忄

笔顺及笔画数　Stroke order and number

| 丶 | 丶 | 忄 | | 3 |
|---|---|---|---|---|
| 忄 | 忄 | 忄 | 忄 | 忄 |

情　qíng　feeling

忄 + 青 = 情

"情"感是种心理活动。
To have feeling is a mental activity.

| 忄 | 忄 | 忄 | 忄 | 忄 | 情 | | | 11 |
|---|---|---|---|---|---|---|---|---|
| 情 | 情 | 情 | 情 | 情 | 情 | 情 | 情 | 情 |

怕　pà　to fear

忄 + 白 = 怕

害"怕"是心理活动。
To fear is a mental activity.

| 忄 | 忄 | 怕 | | | | | | 8 |
|---|---|---|---|---|---|---|---|---|
| 怕 | 怕 | 怕 | 怕 | 怕 | 怕 | 怕 | 怕 | 怕 |

快 kuài pleased, fast 忄 + 夬 = 快

愉"快"是一种心情。
To be pleased is a frame of mind.

| 忄 | 忄 | 忄 | 快 | 快 | | | 7 |
|---|---|---|---|---|---|---|---|
| 快 | 快 | 快 | 快 | 快 | 快 | 快 | 快 | 快 |

慢 màn slow 忄 + 曼 = 慢

"快"和"慢"是人的心理感觉。
The duration of an action may be slow depending on one's frame of mind.

| 忄 | 忄 | 忄 | 愠 | 愠 | 愠 | 愠 | 14 |
|---|---|---|---|---|---|---|---|
| 慢 | 慢 | 慢 | 慢 | 慢 | 慢 | 慢 | 慢 | 慢 |

忙 máng be busy 忄 + 亡 = 忙

"忙"也是人的一种心理感觉。
Being busy can also be a frame of mind.

| 忄 | 忄 | 忙 | 忙 | | | | 6 |
|---|---|---|---|---|---|---|---|
| 忙 | 忙 | 忙 | 忙 | 忙 | 忙 | 忙 | 忙 | 忙 |

惯 guàn be in the habit of 忄 + 贯 = 惯

习"惯"是人的一种心理活动方式。
A habit is a type of subconscious mental activity.

| 忄 | 忄 | 忄 | 惯 | 惯 | 惯 | | 11 |
|---|---|---|---|---|---|---|---|
| 惯 | 惯 | 惯 | 惯 | 惯 | 惯 | 惯 | 惯 | 惯 |

# 【歺部】

歺部的字多和死亡有关。歺字旁在字的左侧。
Characters with the radical 歺 refer to death. It is usually placed on the left side.

歺　　　dǎi　　　　　　　　　　　evil

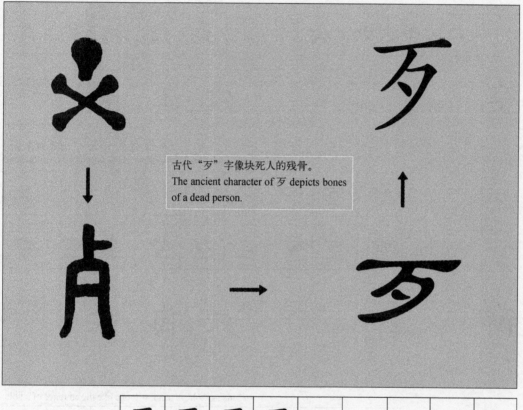

古代"歺"字像块死人的残骨。
The ancient character of 歺 depicts bones of a dead person.

| 一 | 厂 | 歹 | 歺 |  |  |  |  | 4 |
|---|---|---|---|---|---|---|---|---|
| 歺 | 歺 | 歺 | 歺 | 歺 | 歺 | 歺 | 歺 | 歺 |

死　　sǐ　　to die　　　　歹 ＋ 匕 ＝ 死　　

"匕"表示"匕首"。"残骨"加"匕首"表示人已被刺杀而"死"。
匕 means dagger. 歹 shows bones of the dead. Putting together, they form 死, killed by a dagger.

| 歹 | 歹 | 死 |  |  |  |  |  | 6 |
|---|---|---|---|---|---|---|---|---|
| 死 | 死 | 死 | 死 | 死 | 死 | 死 | 死 | 死 |

95

# 【穴部】

穴

称说：穴宝盖

Name: xuébǎogài                    hole

| 丶 | 丷 | 宀 | 宀 | 穴 | | 穴 | 穴 | 穴 | 穴 | 5 |
|---|---|---|---|---|---|---|---|---|---|---|

空   kōng   empty

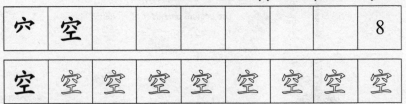

穴 + 工 = 空

"洞穴" 是 "空" 的。"工" 作声旁。
穴 means hole. The hole is empty. 工 is the phonetic component.

| 穴 | 空 | | | | | | | 8 |
|---|---|---|---|---|---|---|---|---|

| 空 | 空 | 空 | 空 | 空 | 空 | 空 | 空 | 空 |
|---|---|---|---|---|---|---|---|---|

窗   chuāng   window

穴 + 囱 = 窗

"窗" 户像 "洞穴" 的口。
穴 means hole. A window looks like the entrance of a hole.

| 穴 | 宀 | 宀 | 宊 | 宊 | 窗 | 窗 | 窗 | 12 |
|---|---|---|---|---|---|---|---|---|

| 窗 | 窗 | 窗 | 窗 | 窗 | 窗 | 窗 | 窗 | 窗 |
|---|---|---|---|---|---|---|---|---|

穿   chuān   to penetrate

穴 + 牙 = 穿

从 "洞穴" 一头走到另一头为 "穿" 行。
穴 means hole. Going from the entrance of a hole to the end is called penetration.

| 穴 | 宀 | 穾 | 穿 | 穿 | | | | 9 |
|---|---|---|---|---|---|---|---|---|

| 穿 | 穿 | 穿 | 穿 | 穿 | 穿 | 穿 | 穿 | 穿 |
|---|---|---|---|---|---|---|---|---|

# 【目部】

目部的字和眼睛有关。目字旁的位置较灵活。
Characters with the radical 目 refer to eyes. Its position is flexible.

目　　　mù　　　　　　　　eye

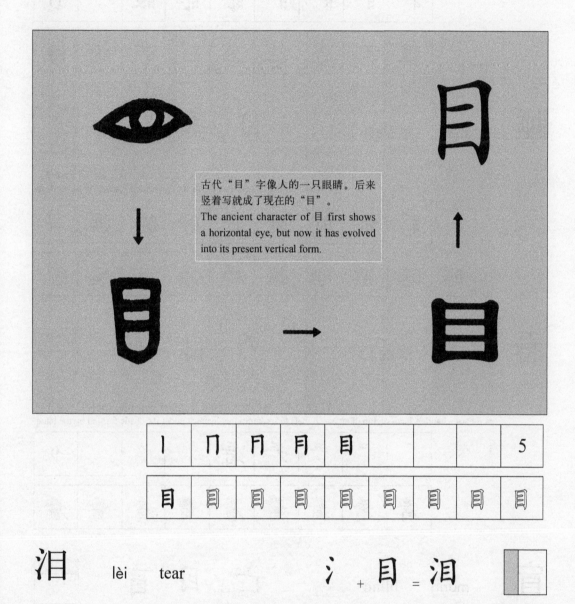

古代"目"字像人的一只眼睛。后来竖着写就成了现在的"目"。
The ancient character of 目 first shows a horizontal eye, but now it has evolved into its present vertical form.

| 丨 | 冂 | 冃 | 目 | 目 | | | | 5 |
|---|---|---|---|---|---|---|---|---|

| 目 | 目 | 目 | 目 | 目 | 目 | 目 | 目 | 目 |
|---|---|---|---|---|---|---|---|---|

泪　　　lèi　　tear　　　　　氵 + 目 = 泪

从"眼睛"中流出的"水"叫"泪"水。
氵 means water. Water running from the eyes is tears.

| 氵 | 泪 | | | | | | | 8 |
|---|---|---|---|---|---|---|---|---|

| 泪 | 泪 | 泪 | 泪 | 泪 | 泪 | 泪 | 泪 | 泪 |
|---|---|---|---|---|---|---|---|---|

97

# 眼　yǎn　eye

目 + 艮 = 眼　

"眼"是个形声字。"艮"作声旁。
目 means eyes. 艮 is the phonetic component.

| 目 | 目丿 | 目卩 | 目卩 | 眼 | 眼 | 眼 | | 11 |
|---|---|---|---|---|---|---|---|---|

| 眼 | 眼 | 眼 | 眼 | 眼 | 眼 | 眼 | 眼 | 眼 |
|---|---|---|---|---|---|---|---|---|

# 睡　shuì　to sleep

目 + 垂 = 睡　

"眼"睑下"垂"是"睡"觉的样子。
垂 means falling. When the eyelids drop, a person is ready to go to sleep.

| 目 | 目丿 | 目丄 | 盱 | 盱 | 眍 | 睡 | 睡 | 睡 | 13 |
|---|---|---|---|---|---|---|---|---|---|

| 睡 | 睡 | 睡 | 睡 | 睡 | 睡 | 睡 | 睡 | 睡 | 睡 |
|---|---|---|---|---|---|---|---|---|---|

# 看　kàn　to look

手 + 目 = 看

"看"是"手"字的变体。手放在"眼睛"上方是"眺望"的样子。
手 means a hand. A hand on top of an eye signals to look into the distance under the shade formed by the hand.

| 一 | 二 | 三 | 手 | 看 | | | | 9 |
|---|---|---|---|---|---|---|---|---|

| 看 | 看 | 看 | 看 | 看 | 看 | 看 | 看 | 看 |
|---|---|---|---|---|---|---|---|---|

# 盲　máng　blind

亡 + 目 = 盲　

"亡"表示死亡。失去视觉就成了"盲"人。
亡 means to die. A man with dead eyes is blind.

| 丶 | 亠 | 亡 | 盲 | | | | | 8 |
|---|---|---|---|---|---|---|---|---|

| 盲 | 盲 | 盲 | 盲 | 盲 | 盲 | 盲 | 盲 | 盲 |
|---|---|---|---|---|---|---|---|---|

# 【田部】

田部的字多和田地、耕作有关。田字旁的位置较灵活。
Characters with the radical 田 refer to the fields and tillage. Its position is flexible.

田　　tián　　　　　　　　　　　　field

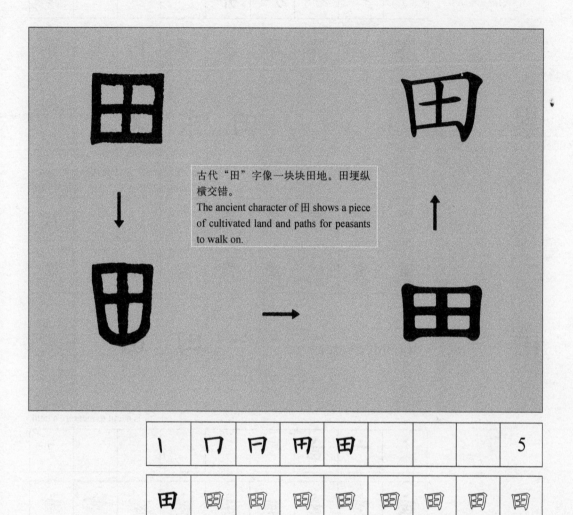

古代"田"字像一块块田地。田埂纵横交错。
The ancient character of 田 shows a piece of cultivated land and paths for peasants to walk on.

| ㇐ | 冂 | 冂 | 冋 | 田 | | | | 5 |
|---|---|---|---|---|---|---|---|---|
| 田 | 田 | 田 | 田 | 田 | 田 | 田 | 田 | 田 |

男　　nán　　man; male　　　　田 + 力 = 男

"力"表示力气。在"田地"里工作的人一般都是"男"人，因为他们有"力气"。
田 means field and 力 means strength. People who work in the fields are generally men because they have more strength.

| 田 | 男 | | | | | | | 7 |
|---|---|---|---|---|---|---|---|---|
| 男 | 男 | 男 | 男 | 男 | 男 | 男 | 男 | 男 |

99

# 界　jiè　boundary

田 + 介 = 界

"田地"都是有边"界"的。"介"作声旁。
The field has a boundary. 介 is the phonetic component.

| 田 | 甼 | 界 | 界 | 界 | | | | 9 |
|---|---|---|---|---|---|---|---|---|
| 界 | 界 | 界 | 界 | 界 | 界 | 界 | 界 | 界 |

# 累　lèi　tired

田 + 糸 = 累

在"田地"里工作是劳"累"的。
A person who works in the field is tired.

| 田 | 毗 | 累 | 累 | 累 | | | | 11 |
|---|---|---|---|---|---|---|---|---|
| 累 | 累 | 累 | 累 | 累 | 累 | 累 | 累 | 累 |

# 亩　mǔ　(a unit of area)

亠 + 田 = 亩

"亩"是丈量"田地"的单位。
亩 is a unit to measure a field.

| 丶 | 亠 | 亩 | | | | | | 7 |
|---|---|---|---|---|---|---|---|---|
| 亩 | 亩 | 亩 | 亩 | 亩 | 亩 | 亩 | 亩 | 亩 |

# 畜　xù　to raise (domestic animals)

玄 + 田 = 畜

在广阔的"田野"才可以发展"畜"牧业。
On a vast land, we can raise livestock.

| 丶 | 亠 | 玄 | 玄 | 畜 | | | | 10 |
|---|---|---|---|---|---|---|---|---|
| 畜 | 畜 | 畜 | 畜 | 畜 | 畜 | 畜 | 畜 | 畜 |

# 【禾部】

禾     hé                    cereal

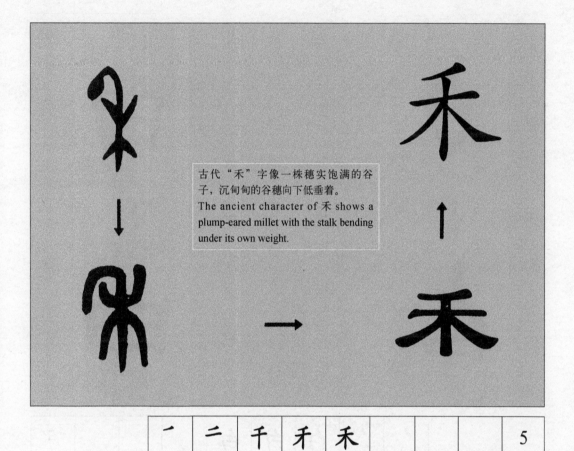

古代"禾"字像一株穗实饱满的谷子，沉甸甸的谷穗向下低垂着。
The ancient character of 禾 shows a plump-eared millet with the stalk bending under its own weight.

| 一 | 二 | 千 | 禾 | 禾 | | | | 5 |
|---|---|---|---|---|---|---|---|---|
| 禾 | 禾 | 禾 | 禾 | 禾 | 禾 | 禾 | 禾 | 禾 |

种     zhòng     to grow, to plant     禾 + 中 = 种   

"禾"表示庄稼。庄稼是"种"植的。"中"作声旁。
禾 shows standing grain. The grain is planted. 中 is the phonetic component.

| 禾 | 和 | 种 | | | | | | 9 |
|---|---|---|---|---|---|---|---|---|
| 种 | 种 | 种 | 种 | 种 | 种 | 种 | 种 | 种 |

# 【白部】

白部的字多和白色、明亮有关。白字旁的位置较灵活。
Characters with the radical 白 refer to white colour or light. Its position is flexible.

白　　bái　　　　　　　　　　　　　white

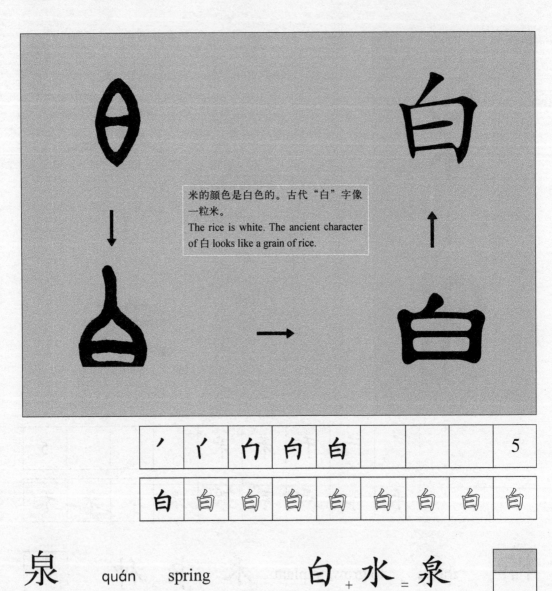

米的颜色是白色的。古代"白"字像一粒米。
The rice is white. The ancient character of 白 looks like a grain of rice.

| ノ | イ | 亇 | 白 | 白 | | | | 5 |
|---|---|---|---|---|---|---|---|---|
| 白 | 白 | 白 | 白 | 白 | 白 | 白 | 白 | 白 |

泉　　quán　　spring　　　　白 + 水 = 泉

"泉"是从地下涌出的"白"花花的"水"。
水 means water. A spring is clear water that gushes out from underground.

| 白 | 泉 | | | | | | | 9 |
|---|---|---|---|---|---|---|---|---|
| 泉 | 泉 | 泉 | 泉 | 泉 | 泉 | 泉 | 泉 | 泉 |

# 【立部】

立部的字多和站立有关。立字旁的位置较灵活。
Most characters with the radical 立 refer to standing. Its position is flexible.

立     lì                                  standing up

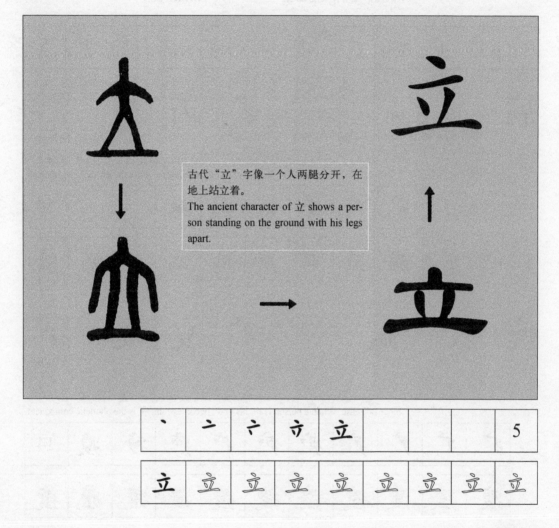

古代"立"字像一个人两腿分开，在地上站立着。
The ancient character of 立 shows a person standing on the ground with his legs apart.

| 、 | 二 | 六 | 立 | 立 | | | 5 |
|---|---|---|---|---|---|---|---|

| 立 | 立 | 立 | 立 | 立 | 立 | 立 | 立 | 立 |
|---|---|---|---|---|---|---|---|---|

站    zhàn    to stand      立 + 占 = 站

"站"是"立"的意思。"占"作声旁。
立 means standing. 占 is the phonetic component.

| 立 | 刘 | 卦 | 站 | | | | 10 |
|---|---|---|---|---|---|---|---|

| 站 | 站 | 站 | 站 | 站 | 站 | 站 | 站 | 站 |
|---|---|---|---|---|---|---|---|---|

# 【疒部】

疒　称说：病字旁

　　Name: bìngzìpáng　　　　sickness

| 、 | ﹀ | 广 | 疒 | 疒 |
|---|---|---|---|---|

| 疒 | 疒 | 疒 | 疒 | 5 |
|---|---|---|---|---|

病　bìng　ill

$$疒 + 丙 = 病$$

"疒"表示疾"病"。"丙"作声旁。
疒 means disease. 丙 is the phonetic component.

| 疒 | 疒 | 疒 | 疒 | 病 | 病 | | | | 10 |
|---|---|---|---|---|---|---|---|---|---|

| 病 | 病 | 病 | 病 | 病 | 病 | 病 | 病 | 病 |
|---|---|---|---|---|---|---|---|---|

瘦　shòu　thin

$$疒 + 叟 = 瘦$$

人有"病"，身体才变得消"瘦"。"叟"作声旁。
疒 means disease. When a person is ill, his body becomes thin. 叟 is the phonetic component.

| 疒 | 疒 | 疒 | 疒 | 疒 | 疒 | 疖 | 瘐 | 瘦 | 瘦 | 14 |
|---|---|---|---|---|---|---|---|---|---|---|

| 瘦 | 瘦 | 瘦 | 瘦 | 瘦 | 瘦 | 瘦 | 瘦 | 瘦 | 瘦 |
|---|---|---|---|---|---|---|---|---|---|---|

疼　téng　to ache; pain

$$疒 + 冬 = 疼$$

"疼"痛是人生"病"以后的一种感觉。"冬"作声旁。
疒 means disease. When a person is ill, he has a pain. 冬 is the phonetic component.

| 疒 | 疒 | 疒 | 疼 | 疼 | 疼 | | | | 10 |
|---|---|---|---|---|---|---|---|---|---|

| 疼 | 疼 | 疼 | 疼 | 疼 | 疼 | 疼 | 疼 | 疼 |
|---|---|---|---|---|---|---|---|---|

# 【皿部】

皿部的字多和器皿有关。皿字底在字的底部。
Characters with the radical 皿 refer to a receptacle. It is usually placed at the bottom.

皿　　mǐn　　　　　　　　　　　　　receptacle

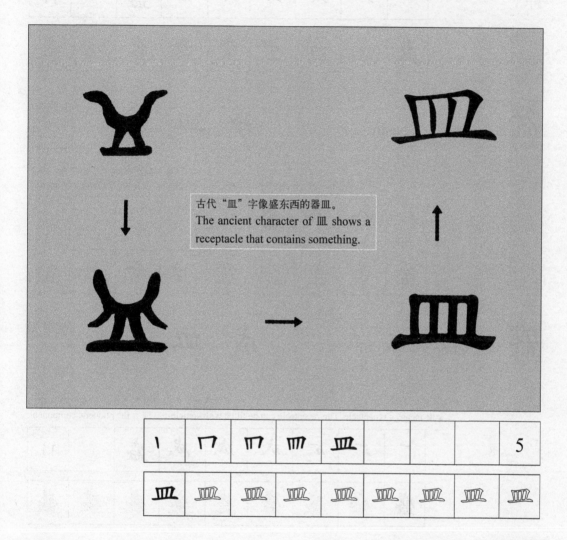

古代"皿"字像盛东西的器皿。
The ancient character of 皿 shows a receptacle that contains something.

| 丶 | 冂 | 冂 | 皿 | 皿 | | | | | 5 |
|---|---|---|---|---|---|---|---|---|---|

| 皿 | 皿 | 皿 | 皿 | 皿 | 皿 | 皿 | 皿 | 皿 | |

盒　hé　box　　　合 + 皿 = 盒

"盒"子具有"器皿"一样的功能。"合"作声旁。
皿 means a receptacle. A box can function as a receptacle. 合 is the phonetic component.

| 亼 | 仌 | 合 | 盒 | | | | | | 11 |
|---|---|---|---|---|---|---|---|---|---|

| 盒 | 盒 | 盒 | 盒 | 盒 | 盒 | 盒 | 盒 | 盒 | |

**盘**    pán    tray, plate

舟 + 皿 = 盘

"盘"子是种器皿。
皿 means a receptacle. A plate is a receptacle.

| ′ | ㇉ | 刀 | 夘 | 舟 | 舟 | 盘 | | | 11 |
|---|---|---|---|---|---|---|---|---|---|
| 盘 | 盘 | 盘 | 盘 | 盘 | 盘 | 盘 | 盘 | 盘 | |

**盆**    pén    basin

分 + 皿 = 盆

"盆"是种器皿。"分"作声旁。
皿 means a receptacle. A basin is a receptacle. 分 is the phonetic component.

| ′ | 八 | 分 | 盆 | | | | | 9 |
|---|---|---|---|---|---|---|---|---|
| 盆 | 盆 | 盆 | 盆 | 盆 | 盆 | 盆 | 盆 | 盆 |

**盛**    chéng    to fill

成 + 皿 = 盛

"器皿"可以"盛"东西。"成"作声旁。
皿 means a receptacle. The receptacle can be filled with something. 成 is the phonetic component.

| 一 | 厂 | 厅 | 成 | 成 | 成 | 盛 | | | 11 |
|---|---|---|---|---|---|---|---|---|---|
| 盛 | 盛 | 盛 | 盛 | 盛 | 盛 | 盛 | 盛 | 盛 | |

**盖**    gài    lid; to cover

羊 + 皿 = 盖

"器皿"有"盖"子。
皿 means a receptacle. The receptacle has a lid.

| ′ | ′′ | ㇓ | ㇓ | ㇓ | 羊 | 盖 | | | 11 |
|---|---|---|---|---|---|---|---|---|---|
| 盖 | 盖 | 盖 | 盖 | 盖 | 盖 | 盖 | 盖 | 盖 | |

106

# 【石部】

石部的字多和石头有关。石字旁一般在字的左侧。
Characters with the radical 石 refer to the stone. It is placed on the left side.

石　shí　　　　　　　　　　　　　stone

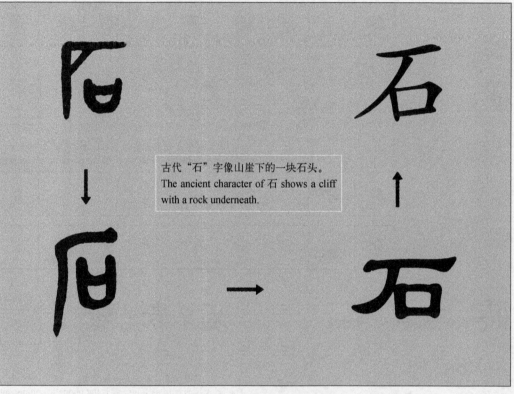

古代"石"字像山崖下的一块石头。
The ancient character of 石 shows a cliff with a rock underneath.

| 一 | 丁 | 石 | 石 | 石 | | | | | 5 |
|---|---|---|---|---|---|---|---|---|---|
| 石 | 石 | 石 | 石 | 石 | 石 | 石 | 石 | 石 | |

碗　wǎn　bowl　　　　　石 + 宛 = 碗　

古代"碗"是用"石"头做的。"宛"作声旁。
In ancient times, bowls were made with stone. 宛 is the phonetic component.

| 石 | 矿 | 碗 | 碗 | 碗 | | | | | 13 |
|---|---|---|---|---|---|---|---|---|---|
| 碗 | 碗 | 碗 | 碗 | 碗 | 碗 | 碗 | 碗 | 碗 | |

107

# 硬 yìng hard, stiff

石 + 更 = 硬

"石"头是坚"硬"的。"更"作声旁。
The stone is hard. 更 is the phonetic component.

| 石 | 石 | 硒 | 硬 | 硬 | | | 12 |
|---|---|---|---|---|---|---|---|
| 硬 | 硬 | 硬 | 硬 | 硬 | 硬 | 硬 | 硬 | 硬 |

# 矿 kuàng mine, ore

石 + 广 = 矿

"矿"是富有开采价值的"石"头。"广"作声旁。
Ore is type of stone containing valuable minerals. 广 is the phonetic component.

| 石 | 矿 | | | | | | 8 |
|---|---|---|---|---|---|---|---|
| 矿 | 矿 | 矿 | 矿 | 矿 | 矿 | 矿 | 矿 | 矿 |

# 砖 zhuān brick

石 + 专 = 砖

"砖"像"石"头一样坚硬。"专"作声旁。
The brick is as hard as stone. 专 is the phonetic component.

| 石 | 石 | 砖 | 砖 | 砖 | | | 9 |
|---|---|---|---|---|---|---|---|
| 砖 | 砖 | 砖 | 砖 | 砖 | 砖 | 砖 | 砖 | 砖 |

# 岩 yán rock

山 + 石 = 岩

"山"上的"石"头叫"岩"石。
山 depicts a mountain, and 石 depicts a stone. The two together mean the stones on the mountain, i.e. rocks.

| 山 | 岩 | | | | | | 8 |
|---|---|---|---|---|---|---|---|
| 岩 | 岩 | 岩 | 岩 | 岩 | 岩 | 岩 | 岩 | 岩 |

# 【示部】

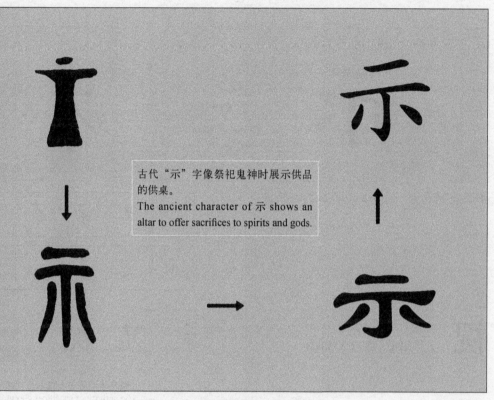

示部的字多和展示的意思有关。示字旁在字的下部。
Characters with the radical 示 refer to display. It is placed at the bottom.

示　　　shì　　　　　　　　　　to show

古代"示"字像祭祀鬼神时展示供品的供桌。
The ancient character of 示 shows an altar to offer sacrifices to spirits and gods.

| 一 | 二 | 〒 | 示 | 示 | | | 5 |
|---|---|---|---|---|---|---|---|
| 示 | 示 | 示 | 示 | 示 | 示 | 示 | 示 | 示 |

票　　piào　ticket　　　　西 + 示 = 票

"票"是要展"示"给人看的东西。
示 means to show. Ticket is a paper to display something.

| 一 | 冖 | 〓 | 西 | 西 | 西 | 票 | 11 |
|---|---|---|---|---|---|---|---|
| 票 | 票 | 票 | 票 | 票 | 票 | 票 | 票 | 票 |

109

# 【礻部】

"礻"是由"示"字演变而来。礻部的字多和祭祀鬼神有关，其位置在字的左侧。

礻 is evolved from 示. Characters with the radical 礻 refer to sacrifices, goods and misfortune. It is placed on the left side.

礻　　　称说：示补旁
　　　　Name: shìbǔpáng　　　　　　show

**笔顺及笔画数**　Stroke order and number

| 、 | 亻 | 礻 | 礻 | 4 |
|---|---|---|---|---|
| 礻 | 礻 | 礻 | 礻 | 礻 |

祝　　zhù　　to wish

礻 + 兄 = 祝

祭祀活动是要表达某种"祝"愿。
The activity of sacrifices shows a wish.

| 礻 | 礻 | 祝 | | | | | 9 |
|---|---|---|---|---|---|---|---|
| 祝 | 祝 | 祝 | 祝 | 祝 | 祝 | 祝 | 祝 |

视　　shì　　to look at

礻 + 见 = 视

"见"表示用眼睛看。"示"作声旁。
见 means to see. 示 is the phonetic component.

| 礻 | 礻 | 礻 | 视 | 视 | | | 8 |
|---|---|---|---|---|---|---|---|
| 视 | 视 | 视 | 视 | 视 | 视 | 视 | 视 |

110

# 【鸟部】

鸟部的字多和飞禽有关。鸟字旁的位置一般在字的右侧。
Characters with the radical 鸟 refer to birds. It is usually placed on the right side.

鸟 [鳥] *niǎo*          bird

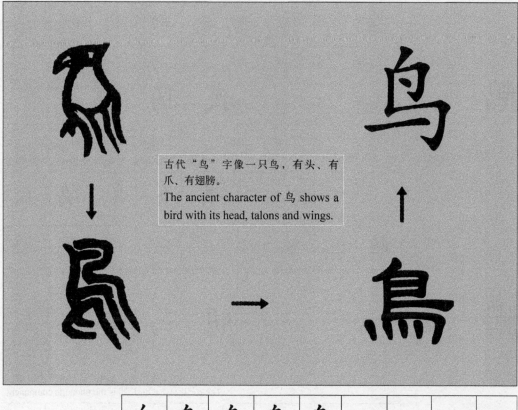

古代"鸟"字像一只鸟，有头、有爪、有翅膀。
The ancient character of 鸟 shows a bird with its head, talons and wings.

| ' | ⺈ | ⺈ | 乌 | 鸟 | | | | 5 |
|---|---|---|---|---|---|---|---|---|
| 鸟 | 鸟 | 鸟 | 鸟 | 鸟 | 鸟 | 鸟 | 鸟 | 鸟 |

鸡    *jī*    chicken        又 + 鸟 = 鸡  

"鸡"是"禽类"。
The chicken is a bird.

| 又 | 鸡 | | | | | | | 7 |
|---|---|---|---|---|---|---|---|---|
| 鸡 | 鸡 | 鸡 | 鸡 | 鸡 | 鸡 | 鸡 | 鸡 | 鸡 |

111

**鸭**    *yā*    duck      甲 + 鸟 = 鸭

"鸭"是"禽类"。"甲"作声旁。
The duck is a bird. 甲 is the phonetic component.

| 丨 | 冂 | 曰 | 日 | 甲 | 鸭 | | | 10 |
|---|---|---|---|---|---|---|---|---|
| 鸭 | 鸭 | 鸭 | 鸭 | 鸭 | 鸭 | 鸭 | 鸭 | 鸭 |

**鹅**    *é*    goose     

"鹅"是"禽类"。"我"作声旁。
The goose is a bird. 我 is the phonetic component.

| ノ | 二 | 于 | 手 | 扎 | 我 | 我 | 鹅 | 12 |
|---|---|---|---|---|---|---|---|---|
| 鹅 | 鹅 | 鹅 | 鹅 | 鹅 | 鹅 | 鹅 | 鹅 | 鹅 |

**鹏**    *péng*    roc      朋 + 鸟 = 鹏

"鹏"是"禽类"。"朋"作声旁。
The roc is also a bird. 朋 is the phonetic component.

| 月 | 朋 | 鹏 | | | | | | 13 |
|---|---|---|---|---|---|---|---|---|
| 鹏 | 鹏 | 鹏 | 鹏 | 鹏 | 鹏 | 鹏 | 鹏 | 鹏 |

**鸣**    *míng*    (of birds) to call, to cry      口 + 鸟 = 鸣

"鸟"用"口"来"鸣叫"。
口 shows mouth. The bird chirps with its mouth.

| 口 | 鸣 | | | | | | | 8 |
|---|---|---|---|---|---|---|---|---|
| 鸣 | 鸣 | 鸣 | 鸣 | 鸣 | 鸣 | 鸣 | 鸣 | 鸣 |

# 【母部】

母部的字中"母"多作声旁。母字旁的位置有的在左侧，有的在字的下部。
In the characters with the radical 母, it is often used as the phonetic component. 母 can be found on the right side or at the bottom.

母　　mǔ　　　　　　　　　　　　　　mother

古代"母"字像胸前有一对乳房跪坐着的妇人。
The ancient character of 母 shows a kneeling woman with her two breasts clearly indicated.

| 乚 | 口 | 马 | 母 | 母 | | | 5 |
|---|---|---|---|---|---|---|---|

| 母 | 母 | 母 | 母 | 母 | 母 | 母 | 母 | 母 |
|---|---|---|---|---|---|---|---|---|

姆　　mǔ　housemaid　　　女 + 母 = 姆　

保"姆"一般都是"女"人。"母"作声旁。
女 means woman. A housemaid is a woman. 母 is the phonetic component.

| 女 | 姆 | | | | | | 8 |
|---|---|---|---|---|---|---|---|

| 姆 | 姆 | 姆 | 姆 | 姆 | 姆 | 姆 | 姆 | 姆 |
|---|---|---|---|---|---|---|---|---|

# 【舟部】

舟　　　　zhōu　　　　　　　　　　　boat

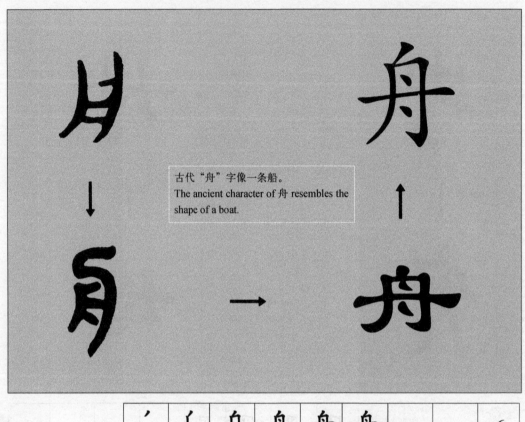

古代"舟"字像一条船。
The ancient character of 舟 resembles the shape of a boat.

| ′ | 丿 | 丿 | 刀 | 舟 | 舟 | | | 6 |
|---|---|---|---|---|---|---|---|---|
| 舟 | 舟 | 舟 | 舟 | 舟 | 舟 | 舟 | 舟 | 舟 |

船　　　chuán　　boat　　　　　舟 + 㕔 = 船　　　

"舟"表示船。
舟 means boat.

| 舟 | 舟 | 舨 | 船 | | | | | 11 |
|---|---|---|---|---|---|---|---|---|
| 船 | 船 | 船 | 船 | 船 | 船 | 船 | 船 | 船 |

# 【虫部】

虫部的字多和爬虫有关。虫字旁的位置一般在字的左侧。
Characters with the radical 虫 refer to insects and reptiles. It is usually placed on the left side.

虫［蟲］ chóng　　　　　　　　　　insect

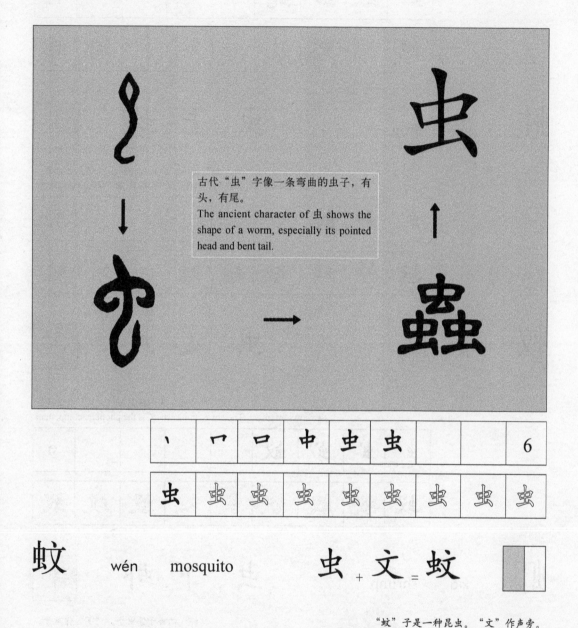

古代"虫"字像一条弯曲的虫子，有头，有尾。
The ancient character of 虫 shows the shape of a worm, especially its pointed head and bent tail.

| 丶 | 丶一 | 口 | 口 | 中 | 虫 | 虫 | | | 6 |
|---|---|---|---|---|---|---|---|---|---|

| 虫 | 虫 | 虫 | 虫 | 虫 | 虫 | 虫 | 虫 | 虫 |
|---|---|---|---|---|---|---|---|---|

蚊　　wén　　mosquito　　　　虫 + 文 = 蚊

"蚊"子是一种昆虫。"文"作声旁。
The mosquito is an insect. 文 is the phonetic component.

| 虫 | 蚊 | | | | | | | 10 |
|---|---|---|---|---|---|---|---|---|

| 蚊 | 蚊 | 蚊 | 蚊 | 蚊 | 蚊 | 蚊 | 蚊 | 蚊 |
|---|---|---|---|---|---|---|---|---|

# 蛇　shé　snake

$$虫 + 它 = 蛇$$

"蛇"是一种爬虫。
虫 shows a reptile. The snake is a reptile.

| 虫 | 虵 | 虼 | 蛇 | | | | 11 |
|---|---|---|---|---|---|---|---|
| 蛇 | 蛇 | 蛇 | 蛇 | 蛇 | 蛇 | 蛇 | 蛇 | 蛇 |

# 蛙　wā　frog

$$虫 + 圭 = 蛙$$

青"蛙"是一种两栖爬行动物，以虫子为食。
虫 shows a reptile. The frog is amphibious and feeds on insects.

| 虫 | 蛀 | 蛙 | | | | 12 |
|---|---|---|---|---|---|---|
| 蛙 | 蛙 | 蛙 | 蛙 | 蛙 | 蛙 | 蛙 | 蛙 | 蛙 |

# 蚁　yǐ　ant

$$虫 + 义 = 蚁$$

蚂"蚁"是一种昆虫。"义"作声旁。
虫 shows an insect. The ant is an insect. 义 is the phonetic component.

| 虫 | 虫 | 虭 | 蚁 | | | | 9 |
|---|---|---|---|---|---|---|---|
| 蚁 | 蚁 | 蚁 | 蚁 | 蚁 | 蚁 | 蚁 | 蚁 | 蚁 |

# 虾　xiā　shrimp

$$虫 + 下 = 虾$$

"虾"的样子像虫子。"下"作声旁。
虫 shows a reptile. The shrimp resembles a reptile. 下 is the phonetic component.

| 虫 | 虫 | 虾 | 虾 | | | | 9 |
|---|---|---|---|---|---|---|---|
| 虾 | 虾 | 虾 | 虾 | 虾 | 虾 | 虾 | 虾 | 虾 |

# 【耳部】

耳部的字多和耳朵有关。耳字旁的位置一般在字的左侧，也有在上下的。

Characters with the radical 耳 refer to the ear. It is usually placed on the left side, sometimes at the top or the bottom.

耳　　　ěr　　　　　　　　ear

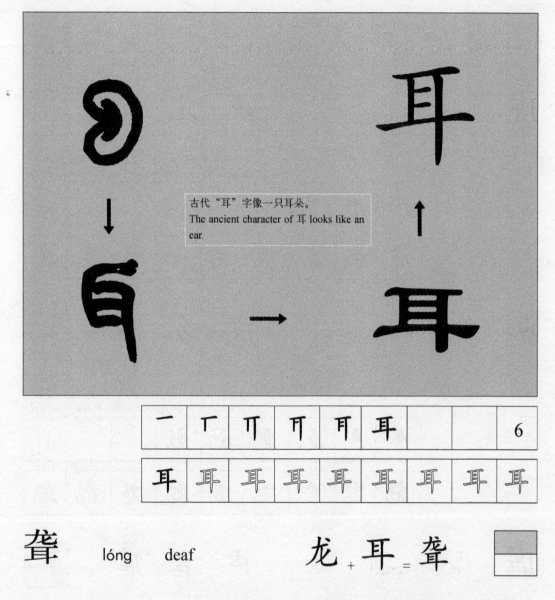

古代"耳"字像一只耳朵。
The ancient character of 耳 looks like an ear.

| 一 | 厂 | 丌 | 丌 | 耳 | 耳 | | | 6 |
|---|---|---|---|---|---|---|---|---|

| 耳 | 耳 | 耳 | 耳 | 耳 | 耳 | 耳 | 耳 | 耳 |
|---|---|---|---|---|---|---|---|---|

聋　　lóng　　deaf　　　　龙 + 耳 = 聋

"耳朵"听不见声音叫"聋"子。"龙"作声旁。
耳 means ear. When the ears do not hear one is deaf. 龙 is the phonetic component.

| 一 | 尢 | 尢 | 龙 | 龙 | 聋 | | | 11 |
|---|---|---|---|---|---|---|---|---|

| 聋 | 聋 | 聋 | 聋 | 聋 | 聋 | 聋 | 聋 | 聋 |
|---|---|---|---|---|---|---|---|---|

117

# 【虍部】

"虍" 部的字有些和虎有关。虎字头在字的上面。
Characters with the radical 虍 refer to the tiger. It is usually placed at the top.

虍     称说：虎字头

        Name: hǔzìpáng         tiger

| ˋ | ⺊ | 上 | 广 | 卢 | 虍 | 6 | | 虍 | 虍 | 虍 |

虎     hǔ     tiger         虍 + 几 = 虎

"虎" 是个象形字。古代虎字像一只老虎的样子。
虎 is a pictogram. The ancient character of 虎 resembles a tiger.

| 卢 | 虏 | 虎 | | | | | | 8 |
| 虎 | 虎 | 虎 | 虎 | 虎 | 虎 | 虎 | 虎 | 虎 |

彪     biāo     a young tiger         虎 + 彡 = 彪

"彪" 是小老虎。
虎 means tiger. 彪 is a young tiger.

| 卢 | 虏 | 虎 | 虎 | 彪 | 彪 | | | 11 |
| 彪 | 彪 | 彪 | 彪 | 彪 | 彪 | 彪 | 彪 | 彪 |

虐     nuè     cruel         虍 + ⺧ = 虐

像 "老虎" 一样残害生灵叫 "虐" 待。
虍 shows a tiger. The way in which the tiger devours an animal is cruel.

| 卢 | 虏 | 虐 | 虐 | | | | | 9 |
| 虐 | 虐 | 虐 | 虐 | 虐 | 虐 | 虐 | 虐 | 虐 |

# 【米部】

米　　　mǐ　　　　　　　　　　　rice

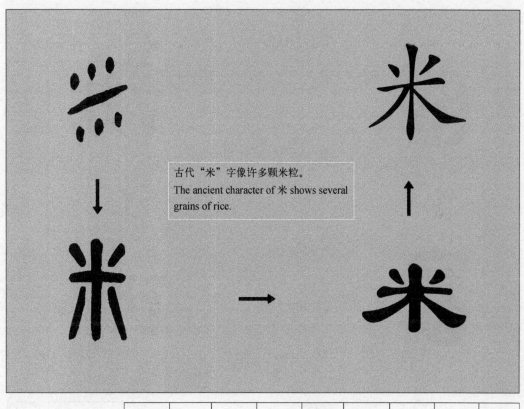

古代"米"字像许多颗米粒。
The ancient character of 米 shows several grains of rice.

| 丶 | 丷 | 丷 | 半 | 米 | 米 | | | 6 |
|---|---|---|---|---|---|---|---|---|

| 米 | 米 | 米 | 米 | 米 | 米 | 米 | 米 | 米 |
|---|---|---|---|---|---|---|---|---|

粮　　liáng　cereal　　　　米 + 良 = 粮

"米"是一种"粮"食。"良"作声旁。
米 shows rice, which is a cereal. 良 is the phonetic component.

| 米 | 米 | 籵 | 籵 | 粁 | 粮 | 粮 | 粮 | 13 |
|---|---|---|---|---|---|---|---|---|

| 粮 | 粮 | 粮 | 粮 | 粮 | 粮 | 粮 | 粮 | 粮 |
|---|---|---|---|---|---|---|---|---|

# 【西部】

西　　　xī　　　　　　　　　　　west

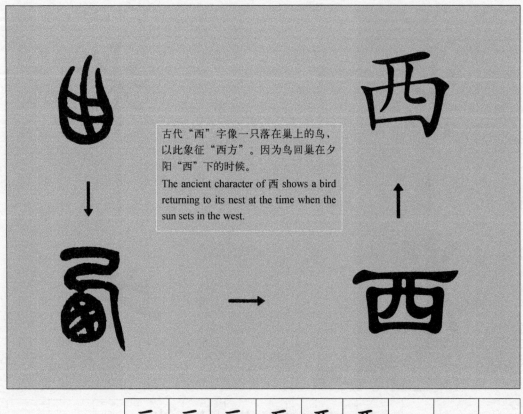

古代"西"字像一只落在巢上的鸟，以此象征"西方"。因为鸟回巢在夕阳"西"下的时候。
The ancient character of 西 shows a bird returning to its nest at the time when the sun sets in the west.

| 一 | 厂 | 冂 | 丙 | 两 | 西 | | 6 |
|---|---|---|---|---|---|---|---|
| 西 | 西 | 西 | 西 | 西 | 西 | 西 | 西 | 西 |

要　　　yào　　to want　　　　　西 + 女 = 要

"要"是个合体字。
要 is a compound character.

| 西 | 要 | | | | | | | 9 |
|---|---|---|---|---|---|---|---|---|
| 要 | 要 | 要 | 要 | 要 | 要 | 要 | 要 | 要 |

120

# 【羊部】

羊部的字多和羊有关。羊字旁的位置较灵活。
Characters with the radical 羊 refer to the sheep. Its position is flexible.

羊　　　yáng　　　　　　　　　　　sheep

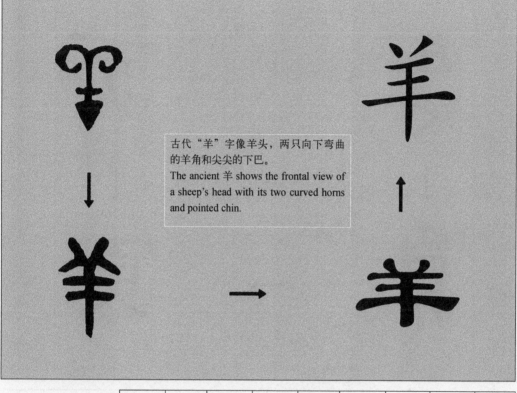

古代"羊"字像羊头，两只向下弯曲的羊角和尖尖的下巴。
The ancient 羊 shows the frontal view of a sheep's head with its two curved horns and pointed chin.

| 、 | ゛ | ゛ | 兰 | 兰 | 羊 | | | 6 |
|---|---|---|---|---|---|---|---|---|
| 羊 | 羊 | 羊 | 羊 | 羊 | 羊 | 羊 | 羊 | 羊 |

美　mĕi　beautiful　　　　羊 ＋ 大 ＝ 美　　

"羊"肥"大"，则肉味鲜"美"。
大 means big. Mutton was man's food in ancient times. If a sheep is big, the mutton is delicious.

| 羊 | 美 | | | | | | | 9 |
|---|---|---|---|---|---|---|---|---|
| 美 | 美 | 美 | 美 | 美 | 美 | 美 | 美 | 美 |

121

# 【页部】

页部的字多和头、颈有关。页字旁的位置一般在字的右侧。
Characters with the radical 页 refer to the head or neck. It is usually placed on the right side.

页 ［頁］ yè　　　　　　　　　　　head, page

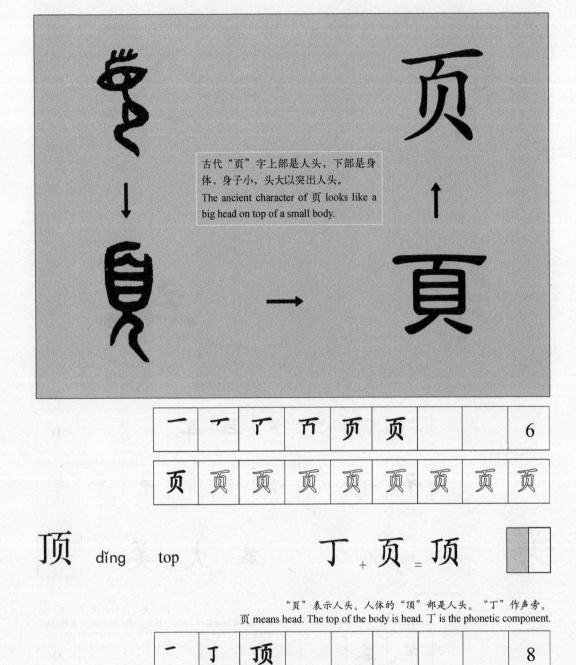

古代"页"字上部是人头，下部是身体，身子小，头大以突出人头。
The ancient character of 页 looks like a big head on top of a small body.

| 一 | 丆 | 丆 | 丆 | 页 | 页 | | | 6 |
|---|---|---|---|---|---|---|---|---|

| 页 | 页 | 页 | 页 | 页 | 页 | 页 | 页 | 页 |
|---|---|---|---|---|---|---|---|---|

顶 dǐng　top　　　　　　丁 + 页 = 顶

"页"表示人头。人体的"顶"部是人头。"丁"作声旁。
页 means head. The top of the body is head. 丁 is the phonetic component.

| 一 | 丁 | 顶 | | | | | | 8 |
|---|---|---|---|---|---|---|---|---|

| 顶 | 顶 | 顶 | 顶 | 顶 | 顶 | 顶 | 顶 | 顶 |
|---|---|---|---|---|---|---|---|---|

# 【衣部】

衣部的字多和衣服有关。衣字旁的位置一般在字的下部或字上下两头。

Characters with the radical 衣 refer to clothes. It is placed at the bottom or divided into two parts.

衣　　yī　　　　　　　　　　　　clothes

古代"衣"字像一件上衣，上面是领子，两边是袖子，下面是下摆。

The ancient character of 衣 shows traditional Chinese upper garment, the uppermost is the collar, the two open sides the sleeves, and the lower-half the lower hem.

| 、 | 一 | 亠 | 衣 | 衣 | 衣 |  | 6 |
|---|---|---|---|---|---|---|---|

| 衣 | 衣 | 衣 | 衣 | 衣 | 衣 | 衣 | 衣 | 衣 |
|---|---|---|---|---|---|---|---|---|

装　zhuāng　clothing　　　壮 + 衣 = 装

"衣"表示服"装"。"壮"作声旁。

衣 means clothes. 壮 is the phonetic component.

| 、 | 丬 | 丬 | 壮 | 壮 | 壮 | 装 | 12 |
|---|---|---|---|---|---|---|---|

| 装 | 装 | 装 | 装 | 装 | 装 | 装 | 装 | 装 |
|---|---|---|---|---|---|---|---|---|

# 【衤部】

"衤"是由"衣"字演变而来的。衤部的字多和衣服有关。衣补旁在字的左侧。
衤 is evolved from 衣. Characters with the radical 衤 also refer to clothes. It is placed on the left side.

衤

称说：衣补旁
Name: yībǔpáng

clothes

笔顺及笔画数　Stroke order and number

| 、 | ラ | ネ | ネ | 衤 | 5 |
|---|---|---|---|---|---|

| 衤 | 衤 | 衤 | 衤 | 衤 | 衤 |
|---|---|---|---|---|---|

衬　　chèn　lining

衤 + 寸 = 衬　

"衤"表示衣服，"衬"是衣服的一部分。"寸"作声旁。
衤 indicates clothes. Lining is part of the clothes. 寸 is the phonetic component.

| 衤 | 衤 | 衬 | 衬 | | | | 8 |
|---|---|---|---|---|---|---|---|

| 衬 | 衬 | 衬 | 衬 | 衬 | 衬 | 衬 | 衬 | 衬 |
|---|---|---|---|---|---|---|---|---|

裤　　kù　trousers

衤 + 库 = 裤　

"裤"子是"服装"的一部分。"库"作声旁。
衤 indicates clothes. Trousers are included in clothing. 库 is the phonetic component.

| 衤 | 衤 | 裤 | | | | | 12 |
|---|---|---|---|---|---|---|---|

| 裤 | 裤 | 裤 | 裤 | 裤 | 裤 | 裤 | 裤 | 裤 |
|---|---|---|---|---|---|---|---|---|

# 【竹部】

竹部的字和竹子有关。竹字旁在合体字中写成"⺮"，其位置在字上部。

Characters with the radical 竹 refer to bamboo. It is usually placed at the top.

竹　　zhú　　　　　　　　　　　　bamboo

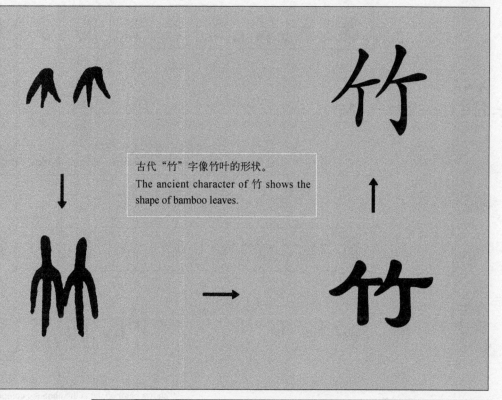

古代"竹"字像竹叶的形状。

The ancient character of 竹 shows the shape of bamboo leaves.

| ノ | ⺍ | 𥫵 | 𥫗 | 𥫗 | 竹 | | | 6 |
|---|---|---|---|---|---|---|---|---|
| 竹 | 竹 | 竹 | 竹 | 竹 | 竹 | 竹 | 竹 | 竹 |

筷　　kuài　　chopsticks　　⺮ + 快 = 筷

中国的"筷"子是用"竹"子做的。"快"作声旁。

⺮ shows bamboo. The chopsticks are made of bamboo. 快 is the phonetic component.

| ⺮ | 𥫗 | 筄 | 笁 | 筷 | 筷 | | | 13 |
|---|---|---|---|---|---|---|---|---|
| 筷 | 筷 | 筷 | 筷 | 筷 | 筷 | 筷 | 筷 | 筷 |

# 筐

**kuāng**    basket      ⺮ + 匡 = 筐

中国古时的"筐"是用"竹子"做的。"匡"作声旁。
⺮ shows bamboo. The baskets are made of bamboo. 匡 is the phonetic component.

| ⺮ | ⺮ | 竺 | 竿 | 竿 | 筐 | 筐 | | 12 |
|---|---|---|---|---|---|---|---|---|

| 筐 | 筐 | 筐 | 筐 | 筐 | 筐 | 筐 | 筐 | 筐 |
|---|---|---|---|---|---|---|---|---|

# 箭

**jiàn**    arrow      ⺮ + 前 = 箭

弓箭的"箭"是用"竹子"做的。"前"作声旁。
⺮ shows bamboo. Arrows are made of bamboo. 前 is the phonetic component.

| ⺮ | ⺮ | 竻 | 笘 | 筲 | 箭 | | | 15 |
|---|---|---|---|---|---|---|---|---|

| 箭 | 箭 | 箭 | 箭 | 箭 | 箭 | 箭 | 箭 | 箭 |
|---|---|---|---|---|---|---|---|---|

# 简

**jiǎn**    bamboo slip      ⺮ + 间 = 简

竹"简"是用"竹子"做的。"间"作声旁。
⺮ shows bamboo. 间 is the phonetic component.

| ⺮ | 竻 | 简 | | | | | | 13 |
|---|---|---|---|---|---|---|---|---|

| 简 | 简 | 简 | 简 | 简 | 简 | 简 | 简 | 简 |
|---|---|---|---|---|---|---|---|---|

# 算

**suàn**    to calculate      ⺮ + 目 + 廾 = 算

中国的"算"盘是用"竹子"做的。
⺮ shows bamboo. The Chinese abacus is made of bamboo.

| ⺮ | 筲 | 筲 | 算 | 算 | | | | 14 |
|---|---|---|---|---|---|---|---|---|

| 算 | 算 | 算 | 算 | 算 | 算 | 算 | 算 | 算 |
|---|---|---|---|---|---|---|---|---|

# 【自部】

自部的字有的和鼻子有关。自字旁的位置一般在字上部。
Some characters composed of the radical 自 relate to the nose. It is usually placed at the top.

自　　　zì　　　　　　　　　　　　self

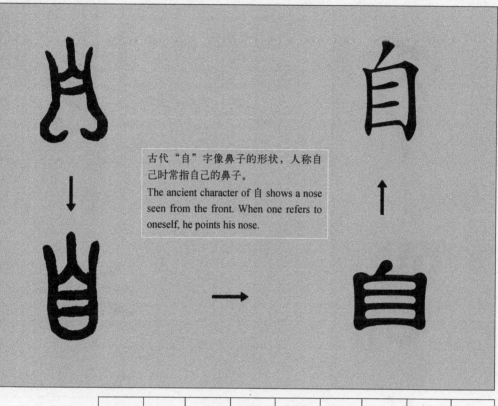

古代"自"字像鼻子的形状，人称自己时常指自己的鼻子。
The ancient character of 自 shows a nose seen from the front. When one refers to oneself, he points his nose.

| ′ | ′ | 冂 | 冃 | 自 | 自 |  |  | 6 |

| 自 | 自 | 自 | 自 | 自 | 自 | 自 | 自 | 自 |

息　　xī　　breath　　　　　　自 ＋ 心 ＝ 息

人喘"息"的时候要用鼻子呼吸，而且此时"心情"也发生变化。
自 indicates nose. 心 means a frame of mind. When a man breathes with his nose his frame of mind may change.

| 自 | 息 |  |  |  |  |  |  | 10 |

| 息 | 息 | 息 | 息 | 息 | 息 | 息 | 息 | 息 |

# 【老部】

老部的字多和年老有关。老字旁的位置一般在字的上部。
Characters with the radical 老 refer to the old age. It is placed at the top.

老 lǎo old

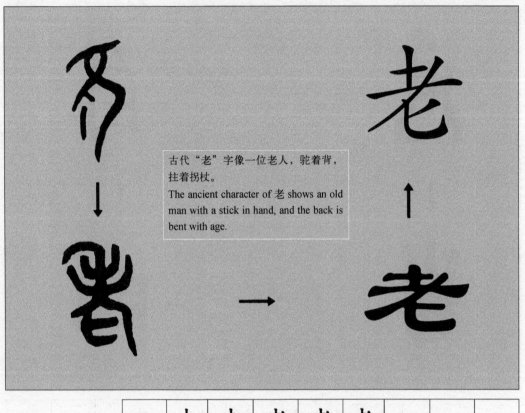

古代"老"字像一位老人，驼着背，拄着拐杖。
The ancient character of 老 shows an old man with a stick in hand, and the back is bent with age.

| 一 | 十 | 土 | 耂 | 耂 | 老 | | | 6 |
|---|---|---|---|---|---|---|---|---|
| 老 | 老 | 老 | 老 | 老 | 老 | 老 | 老 | 老 |

考 kǎo deceased father 耂 + 丂 = 考

"考"表示"老"。死去的父亲一般是老人。
考 indicates old age. The deceased father is normally old.

| 耂 | 耂 | 考 | | | | | | 6 |
|---|---|---|---|---|---|---|---|---|
| 考 | 考 | 考 | 考 | 考 | 考 | 考 | 考 | 考 |

128

# 【走部】

走部的字多和快速行走有关。走字旁在字的左侧。
Characters with the radical 走 refer to quick walking. It is placed on the left side.

走　　　　zǒu　　　　　　　　　　walking

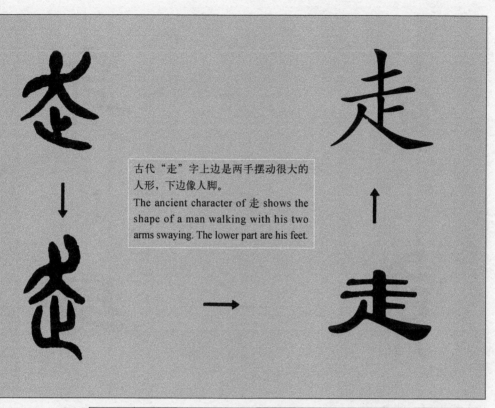

古代"走"字上边是两手摆动很大的人形，下边像人脚。
The ancient character of 走 shows the shape of a man walking with his two arms swaying. The lower part are his feet.

| 一 | 十 | 土 | 卡 | 卡 | 走 | 走 | | 7 |
|---|---|---|---|---|---|---|---|---|

| 走 | 走 | 走 | 走 | 走 | 走 | 走 | 走 | 走 |
|---|---|---|---|---|---|---|---|---|

赶　　　gǎn　　　to catch up with　　　走 + 干 = 赶

很快地"走"才可以追"赶"上前面的人。"干"作声旁。
走 means walking. One who walks quickly can catch up with someone. 干 is the phonetic component.

| 走 | 走 | 走 | 赶 | | | | | 10 |
|---|---|---|---|---|---|---|---|---|

| 赶 | 赶 | 赶 | 赶 | 赶 | 赶 | 赶 | 赶 | 赶 |
|---|---|---|---|---|---|---|---|---|

# 【身部】

身部的字多和身体有关。身字旁的位置一般在字的左侧。
Characters with the radical 身 relate to the body. It is usually placed on the left side.

身　　shēn　　　　　　　　　body

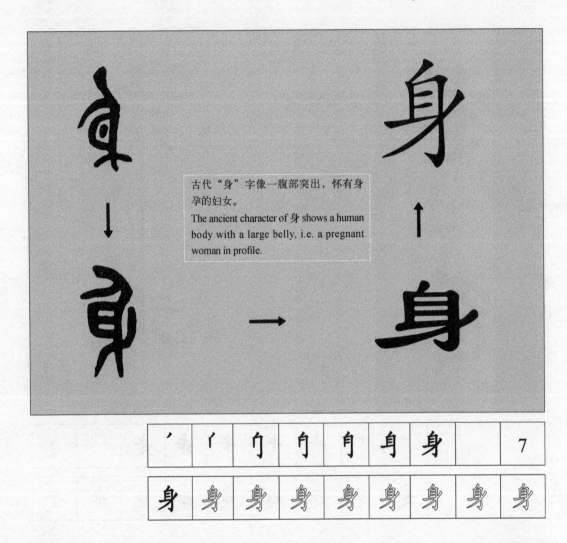

古代"身"字像一腹部突出，怀有身孕的妇女。
The ancient character of 身 shows a human body with a large belly, i.e. a pregnant woman in profile.

| ´ | ⺈ | ⺈ | ⺈ | 自 | 身 | 身 | | | 7 |
|---|---|---|---|---|---|---|---|---|---|
| 身 | 身 | 身 | 身 | 身 | 身 | 身 | 身 | 身 | |

躺　　tǎng　　to lie (down)　　　　身 + 尚 = 躺

"躺"是人身体的一种姿势。"尚"作声旁。
身 means body. To lie down is a posture of the body. 尚 is the phonetic component.

| 身 | 身' | 身' | 躬 | 躺 | | | | | 15 |
|---|---|---|---|---|---|---|---|---|---|
| 躺 | 躺 | 躺 | 躺 | 躺 | 躺 | 躺 | 躺 | 躺 | |

# 【豕部】

豕部的字多和猪有关。豕字旁一般在字的下部或左侧。
Characters with the radical 豕 mostly refer to the pig. It is usually placed at the bottom or on the left side.

豕　　　　　shǐ　　　　　　　　　pig

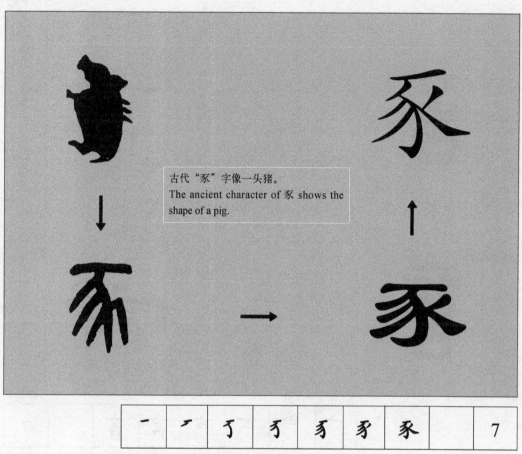

古代"豕"字像一头猪。
The ancient character of 豕 shows the shape of a pig.

| 一 | 丆 | 丆 | 豕 | 豕 | 豕 | 豕 | | 7 |
|---|---|---|---|---|---|---|---|---|
| 豕 | 豕 | 豕 | 豕 | 豕 | 豕 | 豕 | 豕 | 豕 |

家　　jiā　family　　　　宀 + 豕 = 家

"宀"表示房屋，"豕"是猪。在房子周围养猪表示这是一个"家"。
宀 shows house. 豕 means pig. To raise pigs in a house signifies that the house is occupied by a family.

| 宀 | 家 | | | | | | | 10 |
|---|---|---|---|---|---|---|---|---|
| 家 | 家 | 家 | 家 | 家 | 家 | 家 | 家 | 家 |

# 【言部】

言部的字多和言语有关。言字旁的位置一般在字的上面，也有在两侧的。

Characters with the radical 言 refer to language and words. It is usually placed at the top or on the two side.

言    yán             speech, language

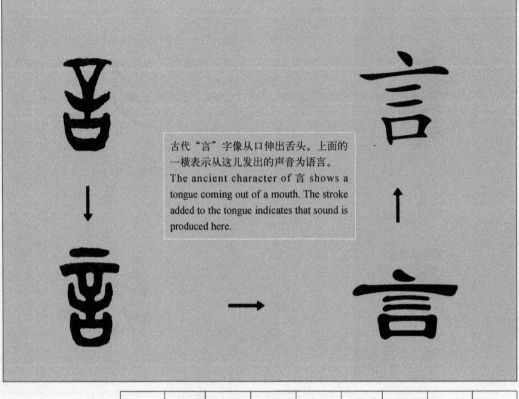

古代"言"字像从口伸出舌头。上面的一横表示从这儿发出的声音为语言。

The ancient character of 言 shows a tongue coming out of a mouth. The stroke added to the tongue indicates that sound is produced here.

| 、 | 一 | 一 | 言 | 言 | 言 | 言 | 7 |
|---|---|---|---|---|---|---|---|
| 言 | 言 | 言 | 言 | 言 | 言 | 言 | 言 | 言 |

信    xìn    letter          亻 + 言 = 信

"信"件传递的是"人"想说的"话"。

言 means language. 人 means human. The language written is a letter.

| 亻 | 信 | | | | | | | 9 |
|---|---|---|---|---|---|---|---|---|
| 信 | 信 | 信 | 信 | 信 | 信 | 信 | 信 | 信 |

# 【讠部】

"讠"是由"言"字演变来的。讠部的字多和言语有关。言字旁在字的左侧。

讠 is evolved from 言. Characters with the radical 讠 relate to language. It is placed on the left side.

讠

称说：言字旁
Name: yánzìpáng

word, language

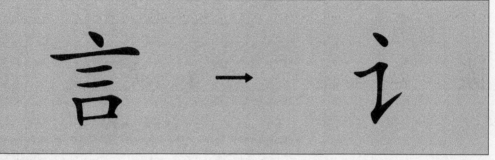

**笔顺及笔画数** Stroke order and number

| 丶 | 讠 | | | | 2 |
|---|---|---|---|---|---|

| 讠 | 讠 | 讠 | 讠 | 讠 |
|---|---|---|---|---|

语　yǔ　language

讠 + 吾 = 语

"讠"表示语言。形声字，"吾"作声旁。
讠 signifies language. 吾 is the phonetic component.

| 讠 | 讠 | 讧 | 语 | 语 | 语 | | | 9 |
|---|---|---|---|---|---|---|---|---|

| 语 | 语 | 语 | 语 | 语 | 语 | 语 | 语 | 语 |
|---|---|---|---|---|---|---|---|---|

说　shuō　to speak

讠 + 兑 = 说

"说"出的东西是"语言"。"兑"作声旁。
讠 signifies word. What a man says is words. 兑 is the phonetic component.

| 讠 | 讠 | 讠 | 说 | 说 | | | | 9 |
|---|---|---|---|---|---|---|---|---|

| 说 | 说 | 说 | 说 | 说 | 说 | 说 | 说 | 说 |
|---|---|---|---|---|---|---|---|---|

**话** huà words

言 + 舌 话

人说"话"的时候"舌"头是要运动的。会意字。
讠signifies words. 舌 means tongue. When a man speaks, his tongue moves.

| 讠 | 讠 | 讠 | 讠 | 话 | | | | 8 |
|---|---|---|---|---|---|---|---|---|
| 话 | 话 | 话 | 话 | 话 | 话 | 话 | 话 | 话 |

**谈** tán to talk

言 + 炎 = 谈

"谈"话是一种言语活动方式。"炎"作声旁。
讠signifies words. To talk we need to use words. 炎 is the phonetic component.

| 讠 | 讠 | 谈 | | | | | | 10 |
|---|---|---|---|---|---|---|---|---|
| 谈 | 谈 | 谈 | 谈 | 谈 | 谈 | 谈 | 谈 | 谈 |

**谢** xiè to thank

言 身 + 寸 谢

对人表示"谢谢"是要说此"话"的。"射"作声旁。
讠signifies words. When we thank someone, we should say some words.

| 讠 | 谢 | 谢 | 谢 | 谢 | | | | 12 |
|---|---|---|---|---|---|---|---|---|
| 谢 | 谢 | 谢 | 谢 | 谢 | 谢 | 谢 | 谢 | 谢 |

**课** kè course, class

言 + 果 课

"课"是需要老师"讲授"的。"果"作声旁。
讠signifies words. When a teacher is in the class, he explains with words. 果 is the phonetic component.

| 讠 | 课 | 课 | | | | | | 10 |
|---|---|---|---|---|---|---|---|---|
| 课 | 课 | 课 | 课 | 课 | 课 | 课 | 课 | 课 |

# 【足部】

足部的字多和脚有关。足字旁的位置不固定。
Characters with the radical 足 relate to the foot. Its position is flexible.

足　　　zú　　　　　　　　　　　leg, foot

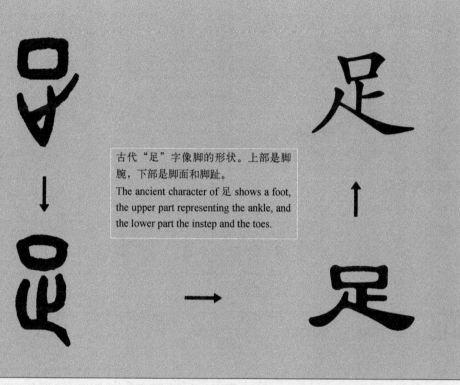

古代"足"字像脚的形状。上部是脚腕，下部是脚面和脚趾。
The ancient character of 足 shows a foot, the upper part representing the ankle, and the lower part the instep and the toes.

| 丶 | 丨 | 口 | 口 | 무 | 무 | 무 | 足 | | 7 |
|---|---|---|---|---|---|---|---|---|---|

| 足 | 足 | 足 | 足 | 足 | 足 | 足 | 足 | 足 |
|---|---|---|---|---|---|---|---|---|

促　　cù　　hurried, urgent　　　亻 + 足 = 促　

急"促"的时候"人"的"脚"步加快。
人 means a person. 足 means foot. When a person is hurried, he quickens his pace.

| 亻 | 促 | | | | | | | | 9 |
|---|---|---|---|---|---|---|---|---|---|

| 促 | 促 | 促 | 促 | 促 | 促 | 促 | 促 | 促 |
|---|---|---|---|---|---|---|---|---|

# 【足部】

"⻊" 是由 "足" 字演变而来。⻊部的字和脚有关，足字旁的位置在字的左侧。

⻊ is evolved from 足. Characters with the radical ⻊ also refer to the foot. It is placed on the left side.

足

称说：足字旁
Name: zúzìpáng

leg, foot

足 → ⻊

**笔顺及笔画数**
Stroke order and number

| ` | ⼝ | 口 | 甲 | 𤴓 | 𧾷 | 足 | 7 |
|---|---|---|---|---|---|---|---|
| 足 | 足 | 足 | 足 | 足 | 足 | 足 | |

跑　pǎo　to run

⻊ + 包 = 跑

"跑" 步要用 "脚"。"包" 作声旁。
⻊ means foot. One uses one's feet to run. 包 is the phonetic component.

| 足 | 𧾷 | 趵 | 跑 | 跑 | 跑 | | 12 |
|---|---|---|---|---|---|---|---|
| 跑 | 跑 | 跑 | 跑 | 跑 | 跑 | 跑 | 跑 | 跑 |

跳　tiào　to jump

⻊ + 兆 = 跳

用 "脚" 来 "跳"。"兆" 作声旁。
⻊ means foot. We use our feet to jump. 兆 is the phonetic component.

| 足 | 𧾷 | 趴 | 跳 | 跳 | 跳 | 跳 | 13 |
|---|---|---|---|---|---|---|---|
| 跳 | 跳 | 跳 | 跳 | 跳 | 跳 | 跳 | 跳 | 跳 |

# 【金部】

金部的字多和金属有关。金字旁的位置一般在字的下部。
Characters with the radical 金 refer to metals. It is usually placed at the bottom.

金　　　jīn　　　　　　　　　　gold, metals

古代"金"字下边是个"土"，表示埋藏在地下的矿藏。
In the ancient character of 金 the lower part is 土 (earth), which shows mineral deposits in the earth.

| ノ | 入 | 人 | 今 | 仐 | 余 | 佘 | 金 | 8 |
|---|---|---|---|---|---|---|---|---|
| 金 | 金 | 金 | 金 | 金 | 金 | 金 | 金 | 金 |

鉴　　　jiàn　　　bronze mirror　　　 + 金 = 鉴

"金"表示金属。"鉴"是铜镜，用铜制作的镜子。
金 signifies metals. The bronze mirror is made of metal.

| 丶 | 丷 | 丷 | 丷 | 丷 | 鉴 | | 13 |
|---|---|---|---|---|---|---|---|
| 鉴 | 鉴 | 鉴 | 鉴 | 鉴 | 鉴 | 鉴 | 鉴 | 鉴 |

# 【钅部】

"钅"是由"金"字演变而来的。钅部的字多和金属有关。钅字旁在字的左侧。

钅 is evolved from 金. Characters with the radical 钅 also refer to metals. It is placed on the left side.

钅　称说：金字旁　　　　　　　　metals
　　Name：jīnzìpáng

**笔顺及笔画数**
Stroke order and number

| ノ | ⺈ | ⻐ | 牟 | 钅 | 5 |
|---|---|---|---|---|---|

| 钅 | 钅 | 钅 | 钅 | 钅 | 钅 |
|---|---|---|---|---|---|

钟　zhōng　clock　　　　钅 + 中 = 钟　

"钅"表示金属，"钟"表是用金属制作的。"中"作声旁。
钅 signifies metals. Metal is used to make a clock. 中 is the phonetic component.

| 钅 | 钅丨 | 钟 | | | | | | 9 |
|---|---|---|---|---|---|---|---|---|

| 钟 | 钟 | 钟 | 钟 | 钟 | 钟 | 钟 | 钟 | 钟 |
|---|---|---|---|---|---|---|---|---|

钱　qián　money　　　　钅 + 戈 = 钱　

"钅"表示金属，古代"钱"币是用金属制作的。"戈"作声旁。
钅 signifies metals. The ancient money was made of metal. 戈 is the phonetic component.

| 钅 | 钅 | 钅丿 | 钱 | 钱 | 钱 | | | 10 |
|---|---|---|---|---|---|---|---|---|

| 钱 | 钱 | 钱 | 钱 | 钱 | 钱 | 钱 | 钱 | 钱 |
|---|---|---|---|---|---|---|---|---|

# 【鱼部】

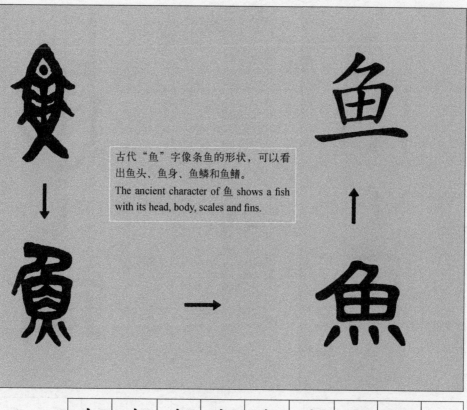

鱼部的字多和鱼有关。鱼字旁的位置较灵活。
Characters with the radical 鱼 relate to the fish. Its position is flexible.

鱼 [魚]　　yú　　　　　　　　　　　　fish

古代"鱼"字像条鱼的形状，可以看出鱼头、鱼身、鱼鳞和鱼鳍。
The ancient character of 鱼 shows a fish with its head, body, scales and fins.

| ノ | ク | ⺈ | 乌 | 乌 | 角 | 鱼 | 鱼 | 8 |
|---|---|---|---|---|---|---|---|---|
| 鱼 | 鱼 | 鱼 | 鱼 | 鱼 | 鱼 | 鱼 | 鱼 | 鱼 |

鲸　　jīng　　whale　　　　　　鱼 + 京 = 鲸　

"鲸"像鱼。"京"作声旁。
鱼 means fish. The whale is thought as a fish. 京 is the phonetic component.

| 鱼 | 鱼` | 鲸 | 鲸 | 鲸 | | | | 16 |
|---|---|---|---|---|---|---|---|---|
| 鲸 | 鲸 | 鲸 | 鲸 | 鲸 | 鲸 | 鲸 | 鲸 | 鲸 |

# 【雨部】

雨　　　yǔ　　　　　　　　　　rain

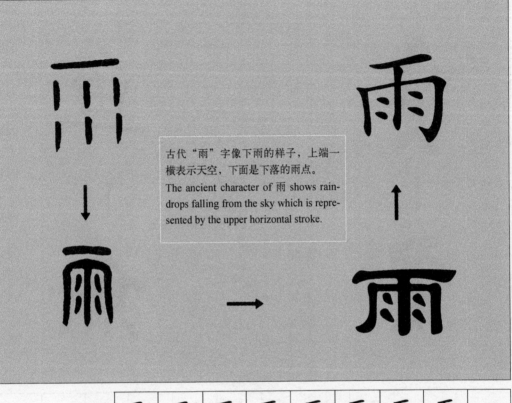

古代"雨"字像下雨的样子，上端一横表示天空，下面是下落的雨点。
The ancient character of 雨 shows raindrops falling from the sky which is represented by the upper horizontal stroke.

| 一 | 厂 | 厅 | 币 | 雨 | 雨 | 雨 | 雨 | 8 |
|---|---|---|---|---|---|---|---|---|
| 雨 | 雨 | 雨 | 雨 | 雨 | 雨 | 雨 | 雨 | 雨 |

雪　　　xuě　　snow　　　　　雨 + 彐 = 雪

"雨"表示下雨。下"雪"也是一种气象。
雨 means rain. Snow, like rain, is also a meteorological phenomenon.

| 雪 | 雪 | 雪 | 雪 | | | | | 11 |
|---|---|---|---|---|---|---|---|---|
| 雪 | 雪 | 雪 | 雪 | 雪 | 雪 | 雪 | 雪 | 雪 |

140

# 【食部】

食部的字多和饮食有关。食字旁一般在字的下部或右侧。
Characters with the radical 食 relate to food. It is usually placed at the bottom or on the right side.

食　　shí　　　　　　　　　　　food

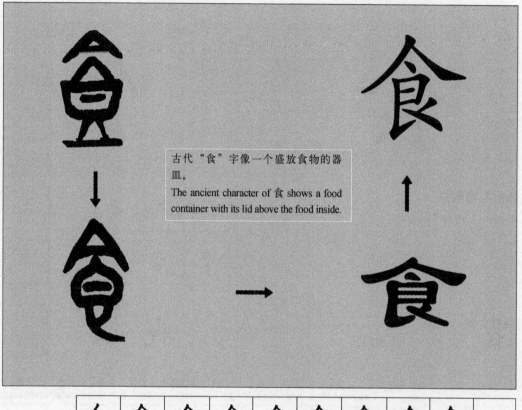

古代"食"字像一个盛放食物的器皿。
The ancient character of 食 shows a food container with its lid above the food inside.

| ノ | 𠆢 | 𠆢 | 今 | 今 | 今 | 食 | 食 | 食 | 9 |
|---|---|---|---|---|---|---|---|---|---|
| 食 | 食 | 食 | 食 | 食 | 食 | 食 | 食 | 食 | 食 |

餐　　cān　　to eat; meal

"餐"是人吃的食物。
食 means food. What a man eats is food or meal.

| ヽ | ト | 歺 | 奴 | 餐 | | | | | 16 |
|---|---|---|---|---|---|---|---|---|---|
| 餐 | 餐 | 餐 | 餐 | 餐 | 餐 | 餐 | 餐 | 餐 | |

141

# 【饣部】

"饣"是由"食"字演变而来的。饣部的字多和饮食有关。饣字旁在字的左侧。

饣 is evolved from 食. Characters with the radical 饣 also refer to food. It is placed on the left side.

饣　称说：食字旁　　　　　　　food
　　Name: shízìpáng

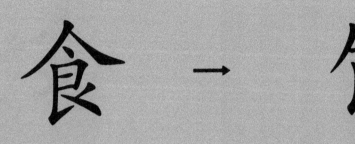

**笔顺及笔画数**
Stroke order and number

| ノ | ㇇ | 饣 | 3 |
|---|---|---|---|

| 饣 | 饣 | 饣 | 饣 | 饣 |
|---|---|---|---|---|

饿　è　hungry　　　　　饣 + 我 = 饿　

"饿"的感觉是想要吃"食物"。"我"作声旁。
饣 signifies food. When one is hungry, he wants to eat food. 我 is the phonetic component.

| 饣 | 饣 | 饣 | 饣 | 饣 | 饿 | 饿 | 饿 | 10 |
|---|---|---|---|---|---|---|---|---|

| 饿 | 饿 | 饿 | 饿 | 饿 | 饿 | 饿 | 饿 | 饿 |
|---|---|---|---|---|---|---|---|---|

饱　bǎo　to be full　　　饣 + 包 = 饱　

"食物"吃够了，就叫"饱"了。"包"作声旁。
饣 signifies food. When one has eaten his full, he cannot eat any more. 包 is the phonetic component.

| 饣 | 饣 | 饣 | 饱 | 饱 | 饱 | | | 8 |
|---|---|---|---|---|---|---|---|---|

| 饱 | 饱 | 饱 | 饱 | 饱 | 饱 | 饱 | 饱 | 饱 |
|---|---|---|---|---|---|---|---|---|

# 【革部】

革部的字多和皮革有关。革字旁的位置一般在字的左侧。
Most characters with the radical 革 relate to leather. It is usually placed on the left side.

革　　　gé　　　　　　　　　leather

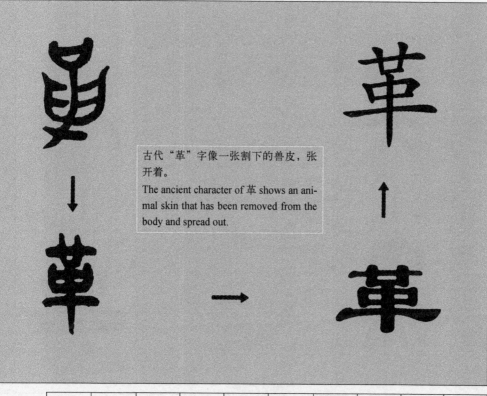

古代"革"字像一张割下的兽皮，张开着。
The ancient character of 革 shows an animal skin that has been removed from the body and spread out.

| 一 | 十 | 艹 | 艹 | 芇 | 苎 | 莒 | 莒 | 革 | 9 |
|---|---|---|---|---|---|---|---|---|---|

| 革 | 革 | 革 | 革 | 革 | 革 | 革 | 革 | 革 | 革 |
|---|---|---|---|---|---|---|---|---|---|

鞋　　xié　shoes　　　　　　　革 + 圭 = 鞋

"鞋"是用皮"革"制作的。
革 means leather. The shoes are made of leather.

| 革 | 鞋 | 鞋 | | | | | | | 15 |
|---|---|---|---|---|---|---|---|---|---|

| 鞋 | 鞋 | 鞋 | 鞋 | 鞋 | 鞋 | 鞋 | 鞋 | 鞋 |
|---|---|---|---|---|---|---|---|---|

# 【黑部】

黑      hēi                black

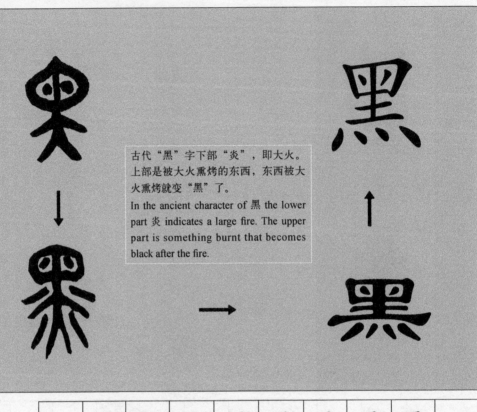

古代"黑"字下部"炎"，即大火。上部是被大火熏烤的东西，东西被大火熏烤就变"黑"了。
In the ancient character of 黑 the lower part 炎 indicates a large fire. The upper part is something burnt that becomes black after the fire.

| 丶 | 冂 | 冎 | 冊 | 四 | 甲 | 甲 | 垔 | 黑 | 12 |
|---|---|---|---|---|---|---|---|---|---|
| 黑 | 黑 | 黑 | 黑 | 黑 | 黑 | 黑 | 黑 | 黑 | 黑 |

墨    mò    Chinese ink        黑 + 土 = 墨

中国人写毛笔字时用的"墨"在研磨之前像一种"黑"色的"土"。
土 means soil. Chinese ink used in painting and calligraphy is like black earth before it is mixed with water.

| 黑 | 墨 | | | | | | | | 15 |
|---|---|---|---|---|---|---|---|---|---|
| 墨 | 墨 | 墨 | 墨 | 墨 | 墨 | 墨 | 墨 | 墨 | |

144

写出下列汉字的部首：Write the radicals of the following characters:

| | | | | | | | | |
|---|---|---|---|---|---|---|---|---|
| 1 | 令【　部】 | 28 | 狮【　部】 | 55 | 界【　部】 |
| 2 | 净【　部】 | 29 | 屎【　部】 | 56 | 针【　部】 |
| 3 | 侨【　部】 | 30 | 嫁【　部】 | 57 | 秋【　部】 |
| 4 | 元【　部】 | 31 | 孝【　部】 | 58 | 鸽【　部】 |
| 5 | 延【　部】 | 32 | 红【　部】 | 59 | 粉【　部】 |
| 6 | 对【　部】 | 33 | 驴【　部】 | 60 | 聪【　部】 |
| 7 | 召【　部】 | 34 | 煮【　部】 | 61 | 蝶【　部】 |
| 8 | 务【　部】 | 35 | 斓【　部】 | 62 | 笛【　部】 |
| 9 | 怪【　部】 | 36 | 炉【　部】 | 63 | 舰【　部】 |
| 10 | 潮【　部】 | 37 | 怎【　部】 | 64 | 跟【　部】 |
| 11 | 记【　部】 | 38 | 祖【　部】 | 65 | 雷【　部】 |
| 12 | 原【　部】 | 39 | 球【　部】 | 66 | 鲜【　部】 |
| 13 | 划【　部】 | 40 | 楼【　部】 | 67 | 爹【　部】 |
| 14 | 完【　部】 | 41 | 歼【　部】 | 68 | 毯【　部】 |
| 15 | 应【　部】 | 42 | 较【　部】 | 69 | 躯【　部】 |
| 16 | 连【　部】 | 43 | 晒【　部】 | 70 | 起【　部】 |
| 17 | 场【　部】 | 44 | 员【　部】 | 71 | 虑【　部】 |
| 18 | 劳【　部】 | 45 | 物【　部】 | 72 | 预【　部】 |
| 19 | 奇【　部】 | 46 | 掌【　部】 | 73 | 百【　部】 |
| 20 | 抗【　部】 | 47 | 版【　部】 | 74 | 亲【　部】 |
| 21 | 堂【　部】 | 48 | 所【　部】 | 75 | 改【　部】 |
| 22 | 吹【　部】 | 49 | 肥【　部】 | 76 | 氖【　部】 |
| 23 | 围【　部】 | 50 | 窄【　部】 | 77 | 馆【　部】 |
| 24 | 帕【　部】 | 51 | 疯【　部】 | 78 | 队【　部】 |
| 25 | 很【　部】 | 52 | 袖【　部】 | 79 | 盐【　部】 |
| 26 | 参【　部】 | 53 | 泵【　部】 | 80 | 岩【　部】 |
| 27 | 岁【　部】 | 54 | 眠【　部】 | | |

如果你不知道一个汉字的发音，可以使用汉语字典中的部首检字法来查找汉字。 我们以从《现代汉词字典》 （第6版）中查找 "婶" 字为例来介绍一下查字典的步骤。

一、 先确定所查汉字的部首。"婶" 字的部首是 "女"。

二、 数一下部首的笔画数。"女" 是三画。

三、 在字典《部首目录》的三画部首中找到"女"，以确定【女部】在第32页上。

四、 根据部首序号，在后面的 《检字表》 中找到 【女部】 。

五、 看所查汉字，除去部首以外，另一部分是多少笔画。 "审" 是8画。

六、 在【女部】的8画中找到"婶"字，知道 "婶" 字在字典中的页码 （1158） 。

七、 根据页码，找到所要查的汉字。

# How to Consult a Chinese Dictionary Using Radical Index

If you don't know the pronunciation of a Chinese character, you can look it up in the dictionary by means of the radical index. This procedure can be followed when consulting most Chinese dictionaries. Here is an example, using *Modern Chinese Dictionary* (《现代汉语词典》, Sixth Edition) to search for the character 婶:

1. First you must determine which part of the character is the radical. In this case, the radical of 婶 is 女.

2. Then count the number of strokes of the radical. 女 has three strokes.

3. Locate the radical 女 under the boldfaced subheading 三画 in (一)部首目录 (Radical Index) and you can see that the radical 女 is on page 32.

4. In the middle of this page you will find 女部, which is listed in (二) 检字表.

5. Then count the strokes of the character apart from the radical. 审 has eight strokes.

6. Under the boldfaced subheading 八画 in 女部 there is the character 婶, with the page number 1158.

7. You will find the character on the page as indicated.

# Index of the Strokes and Radicals
## 部首笔画索引

# •图书推荐•
## Recommendations

## HSK 规范教程（1、2、3、4、5、6 级）

Level 1 : ISBN 9787513807920 ￥49.00　　Level 2 : ISBN 9787513807944 ￥49.00　　Level 3 : ISBN 9787513808026 ￥49.00
Level 4: ISBN 9787513808033 ￥59.00　　Level 5(I): ISBN 9787513808040 ￥49.00　　Level 5(II): ISBN 9787513808040 ￥59.00
Level 6(I): ISBN 9787513810128 ￥59.00　　Level 6(II): ISBN 9787513810135 ￥59.00　　Level 6(III): ISBN 9787513810142 ￥59.0

### HSK 分频词汇
### Frequency-based HSK Vocabulary

汉英 Chinese-English edition
Level 1-3: ISBN 9787513810081 ￥39.00
Level 4: ISBN 9787513810098 ￥29.00
Level 5: ISBN 9787513810104 ￥49.00
Level 6: ISBN 9787513810111 ￥79.00

汉法 Chinese-French edition
汉西 Chinese-Spanish edition
汉韩 Chinese-Korean edition
汉泰 Chinese-Thai edition
汉阿 Chinese-Arabic edition
汉日 Chinese-Japanese edition
汉俄 Chinese-Russian edition

## 新 HSK 模拟试卷及解析（1、2、3、4、5、6 级）

Level 1: ISBN 9787513803366 ￥49.00
Level 2: ISBN 9787513803359 ￥49.00
Level 3: ISBN 9787513803342 ￥49.00
Level 4: ISBN 9787513800853 ￥49.00
Level 5: ISBN 9787513800266 ￥49.00
Level 6: ISBN 9787513800860 ￥68.00

### HSK 词汇练习册
### HSK Vocabulary Workbook

汉英 Chinese-English edition
Level 4: ISBN 9787513811965 ￥25.00
Level 5: ISBN 9787513811972 ￥39.00

For more information, visit us at www.sinolingua.com.cn
**Email:** hyjx@sinolingua.com.cn　**Tel:** 0086-10-68320585, 68997826

# •图书推荐•
# Recommendations

## 汉语语言文字启蒙（共2册）

A Key to Chinese Speech and Writing(2 volumes)

汉英Chinese-English edition

Volume 1: ISBN 9787800525070 ￥75.00

Volume 2:ISBN9787800525087 ￥70.00

## 画说汉字（共两册）

Chinese Characters in Pictures （2volumes）

汉英Chinese-English edition

Volume 1:ISBN 9787802001015

Volume 2：ISBN 9787802001022

￥39.80/each

## 汉字字源入门

The Origins of Chinese Characters

汉法 Chinese-French edition

ISBN 9787800522987

汉德 Chinese-German edition

ISBN 9787800523281

￥40.00/each

## 外国人汉字速成

500 Basic Chinese Characters—A Speedy Elementary Course

汉英Chinese-English edition

ISBN 9787800524608

￥89.50

For more information, visit us at www.sinolingua.com.cn

**Email:** hyjx@sinolingua.com.cn, **Tel:** 0086-10-68320585, 68997826

# ·图书推荐·
## Recommendations

## 商贸汉语系列教材（共 10 册）
### Business Chinese Series (10 volumes)

**商贸汉语阅读与表达 1**
**Reading and Communicating 1**
ISBN 9787513803649
￥59.00

**商贸汉语阅读与表达 2**
**Reading and Communicating 2**
ISBN 9787513803632
￥59.00

**商贸汉语阅读与表达 3**
**Reading and Communicating 3**
ISBN 9787513803618
￥59.00

**商贸汉语阅读与表达 4**
**Reading and Communicating 4**
ISBN 9787513803625
￥49.00

**商贸汉语阅读与表达 5**
**Reading and Communicating 5**
ISBN 9787513801775
￥59.90

**商贸汉语阅读与表达 6**
**Reading and Communicating 6**
ISBN 9787513803991
￥59.00

**商务口语流利说**
**Speak Business Chinese Fluently**
ISBN 9787513803144
￥49.00

**商务汉语写作教程**
**A Chinese Business Writing Course**
ISBN 9787513806169
￥49.00

**汉语应用文写作教程**
**A Practical Chinese Writing Course**
ISBN 9787513802987
￥49.00

**中国文化读本**
**Glimpse into Chinese Culture**
ISBN 9787802009783
￥59.00

For more information, visit us at www.sinolingua.com.cn
Email: hyjx@sinolingua.com.cn  Tel: 0086-10-68320585, 68997826

责任编辑：贾寅淮 郁 苓 陆 瑜
封面设计：禹 田

《新编基础汉语·写字篇》
常用汉字部首

张朋朋 著

*

©华语教学出版社有限责任公司
华语教学出版社有限责任公司出版
（中国北京百万庄大街24号 邮政编码100037）
电话: (86)10-68320585, 68997826
传真: (86)10-68997826, 68326333
网址：www.sinolingua.com.cn
电子信箱：hyjx@sinolingua.com.cn
北京京华虎彩印刷有限公司印刷
2001 年（16 开）第 1 版
2018 年第 1 版第 14 次印刷
（汉英）
ISBN 978-7-80052-576-6
定价：27.00元